THE FRIENDSHIP OF CHRIST

ROBERT HUGH BENSON

THE FRIENDSHIP OF CHRIST

THE CENACLE PRESS
AT SILVERSTREAM PRIORY

Nihil Obstat

REMIGIUS LAFORT, D.D., Censor.

Imprimatur

JOHN CARDINAL FARLEY, Archbishop of New York.

NEW YORK, February 28, 1912.

This edition is based on the 1912 printing by Longmans, Green, and Co. Design of this edition © 2022 Silverstream Priory

The text of *The Friendship of Christ* is in the public domain. All reservable rights reserved for the new material of this edition. No part of the new material of this edition may be reproduced or transmitted, in any form or by any means, without permission.

The Cenacle Press at Silverstream Priory
Silverstream Priory
Stamullen, County Meath, K32 T189, Ireland
www.cenaclepress.com

ppr 978-1-915544-03-2
cloth 978-1-915544-04-9
ebook 978-1-915544-05-6

Book and cover design by Enrique J. Aguilar in collaboration with The Cenacle Press.

The following pages contain in an abbreviated form sermons preached in Rome in the Church of St. Silvestro-in-Capite, during the year of 1911. Some of them were also preached in the Carmelite Church in Kensington in 1910; and all of them, with others, in the Church of our Lady of Lourdes, New York, in 1912. The author apologises for the very much compressed form in which they are printed here; but he has sought to suggest rather than to develop the thoughts of which he treats.

CONTENTS

THIS IS MY FRIEND — 8

PART I: CHRIST IN THE INTERIOR SOUL

THE FRIENDSHIP OF CHRIST (General) —*GEN. ii: 18.* — 9

THE FRIENDSHIP OF CHRIST (Interior) —*GEN. ii: 18.* — 16

THE PURGATIVE WAY —*PSALM l: 4.* — 21

THE ILLUMINATIVE WAY —*PSALM xvii: 29.* — 28

PART II: CHRIST IN THE EXTERIOR

CHRIST IN THE EUCHARIST —*JOHN vi: 35.* — 35

CHRIST IN THE CHURCH —*JOHN xv: 5.* — 42

CHRIST IN THE PRIEST —*JOHN i: 17.* — 49

CHRIST IN THE SAINT —*MATT. v: 14.* — 56

CHRIST IN THE SINNER —*LUKE xv: 2.* — 62

CHRIST IN THE AVERAGE MAN —*MATT. xxv: 40.* — 67

CHRIST IN THE SUFFERER —*Coloss. i: 24.* — 73

PART III: CHRIST IN HIS HISTORICAL LIFE

THE SEVEN WORDS Christ our Friend Crucified — 79

EASTER DAY Christ Our Friend Vindicated —*JOHN xx: 17.* — 109

THIS IS MY FRIEND[1]

Let me tell you how I made His acquaintance.
   I had heard much of Him, but took no heed.
   He sent daily gifts and presents, but I never thanked Him.
   He often seemed to want my friendship, but I remained cold.
   I was homeless, and wretched, and starving and in peril every hour; and He offered me shelter and comfort and food and safety; but I was ungrateful still.
   At last He crossed my path and with tears in His eyes
   He besought me saying, Come and abide with me.
Let me tell you how he treats me now.
   He supplies all my wants.
   He gives me more than I dare ask.
   He anticipates my every need.
   He begs me to ask for more.
   He never reminds me of my past ingratitude.
   He never rebukes me for my past follies.
Let me tell you further what I think of Him.
   He is as good as He is great.
   His love is as ardent as it is true.
   He is as lavish of His promises as He is faithful in keeping them.
   He is as jealous of my love as He is deserving of it.
   I am in all things His debtor, but He bids me call Him Friend.

---

[1] From an old manuscript.

PART I: CHRIST IN THE INTERIOR SOUL

1

THE FRIENDSHIP OF CHRIST

(General)

It is not good for man to be alone.—GEN. ii: 18.

THE EMOTION OF FRIENDSHIP IS AMONGST the most mighty and the most mysterious of human instincts. Materialistic philosophers delight in tracing even the most exalted emotions—art, religion, romance—to purely carnal sources; to the instincts of the propagation or sustentation of physical life; and yet in this single experience at any rate—when we class together, as we can, all those varied relationships between men and men, women and women, as well as between men and women, under the common title of friendship—materialistic philosophy wholly breaks down. It is not a manifestation of sex, for David can cry to Jonathan "Thy love to me was wonderful, passing the love of women"; it is not a sympathy arising from common interests, for the sage and the fool can form a friendship at least as strong as any between two sages or two fools; it is not a relationship based on the exchange of ideas, for the deepest friendships thrive better in silence than in speech. "No man is truly my friend," says Maeterlinck, "until we have each learned to be silent in one another's company."

And this mysterious thing is as mighty as it is mysterious. It is bound to rise, so far as it is true to the laws of its own development, to a pitch of passion far beyond that of ordinary relations between the sexes. Since it is independent of those physical elements necessary to a love between husband and wife, it can rise mysteriously higher in certain respects, than the plane which those elements sustain. It seeks to win nothing, to produce nothing—but to sacrifice all. Even, where the supernatural motive is apparently absent, it can reflect on the natural plane, even more clearly than does sacramental wedded love, the characteristics of divine charity. On its own plane, it also "beareth all things, believeth all things, hopeth all things…seeketh not her own… is not puffed up."[2] It is the salt of perfect matrimony, but it can exist without sex. It takes its place with those other supreme departments of human experience—art, chivalry and even religion—and it is not the least noble of the company.

On the other hand, there is hardly any experience more subject to disillusionment. It deifies beasts, and is disappointed to find them human after all. When my friend fails me at a crisis or when I fail my friend, there is hardly any bitterness in life so bitter. And, again; while friendship itself has an air of eternity about it, seeming to transcend all natural limits, there is hardly any emotion so utterly at the mercy of time. We form friendships, and grow out of them. It might almost be said that we cannot retain the faculty of friendship unless we are continually making new friends: just as, in religion, in proportion as we form inadequate images and ideas of the divine which for the time we adore, and presently change for others, we progress in the knowledge of the True God. I cannot retain true Childhood unless I am continually putting away childish things.

Here then is one of the more princely passions which, while feeding upon earthly things are continuously dissatisfied with them; which, themselves white-hot, are never consumed—one of the passions that make history, and therefore look always to the future and not to the past—a passion which, perhaps above all others, since in its instance it is impossible to resolve it into earthly elements, points to eternity only for the place of its satisfaction, and to the Divine Love for the answering of its human needs. There is but one intelligible explanation then for the desires which it generates yet never fulfils; there is but one supreme friendship to which all human friendships point; one Ideal Friend in whom we find perfect and complete that for which we look

---

[2] 1 Cor. xiii.

in type and shadow in the faces of our human lovers.

I. It is at once the privilege and the burden of Catholics that they know so much of Jesus Christ. It is their privilege, since an intelligent knowledge of the Person and the attributes and the achievements of Incarnate God is an infinitely greater wisdom than all the rest of the sciences put together. To have a knowledge of the Creator is incalculably a more noble thing than to have a knowledge of His Creation. Yet it is a burden as well; for the splendour of this knowledge may be so great as to blind us to the value of its details. The blaze of the Divinity to him who sees it may be so bright as to bewilder him with regard to the humanity. The unity of the wood vanishes in the perfection of the trees.

Catholics then, above all others, are prone—through their very knowledge of the mysteries of faith, through their very apprehension of Jesus Christ as their God, their High Priest, their Victim, their Prophet and their King—to forget that His delights are to be with the sons of men more than to rule the Seraphim, that, while His Majesty held Him on the throne of His Father, His Love brought Him down on pilgrimage that He might transform His servants into His friends. For example, devout souls often complain of their loneliness on earth. They pray, they frequent the sacraments, they do their utmost to fulfil the Christian precepts; and, when all is done, they find themselves solitary. There could scarcely be a more evident proof of their failure to understand one at least of the great motives of the Incarnation. They adore Christ as God, they feed on Him in Communion, cleanse themselves in His precious Blood, look to the time when they shall see Him as their Judge; yet of that intimate knowledge of and companionship with Him in which the Divine Friendship consists, they have experienced little or nothing. They long, they say, for one who can stand by their side and upon their own level, who can not merely remove suffering, but can himself suffer with them, one to whom they can express in silence the thoughts which no speech can utter; and they seem not to understand that this is the very post which Jesus Christ Himself desires to win, that the supreme longing of His Sacred Heart is that

He should be admitted, not merely to the throne of the heart or to the tribunal of conscience, but to that inner secret chamber of the soul where a man is most himself, and therefore most utterly alone.

See how full are the Gospels of this desire of Jesus Christ! There were indeed splendid moments when the God within the Humanity blazed out in glory—moments when the very garments that He wore burned radiant in His Divinity: there were moments of Divine energy when blind eyes opened through creative to created light, when ears deaf to earthly noises heard the Divine Voice, when the dead burst their graves to look on Him who had first given and then restored their life. And there were august and terrible moments when God went apart with God into the wilderness or the garden, when God cried through the lips of desolated humanity, "Why hast Thou forsaken Me?" But for the most part it is of His Humanity that the Gospels tell us; a Humanity that cried to Its kind—a Humanity not only tempted but also, as it were, specialized in all points like as we are. "Now Jesus loved Martha, and her sister Mary, and Lazarus."[3] "Jesus, looking upon him, loved him"[4]—loved him it seems with an emotion distinguished from that of the Divine Love that loves all things that It has made; loved him for the ideal which he in particular might yet accomplish, more than for the fact that he merely existed as did others of his kind— loved him as I love my own friend, and as he loves me.

It is these moments, probably, above all others, that have endeared Jesus Christ to humanity—moments in which He displayed Himself as truly one of us. It is when He is "lifted up"—not in the glory of triumphant Divinity, but in the shame of beaten Humanity, that He draws us to Himself. We read of His works of power and are conscious of awe and adoration: but when we read how He sat weary at the well-side while His friends went for food; how in the Garden, He turned in agonized reproach to those from whom He had hoped for consolation—"What? Could you not watch one hour with Me?"[5]— when He turned once more and for the last time used the sacred

---

[3] John xi: 5.
[4] Mark x: 21.

name to him who had forfeited it for ever—"*Friend*, whereto art thou come?"[6]—we are conscious of that which is even dearer to Him than all the adoration of all the angels in glory—tenderness and love and compassion—emotions to which friendship alone has a right.

Or again;—Jesus Christ speaks to us more than once in the Scripture, not merely in hint and implication, but in deliberate statement, of this desire of His to be our friend. He sketches for us a little picture of the lonely house at nightfall, of Himself who stands and knocks upon the door and of the intimate little meal He expects. "And if any man will open—(any man!)—I will come in to him and will sup with him and he with Me."[7] Or again, he tells those whose hearts are sick at the bereavement that comes upon them so swiftly, "I will not now call you servants…; but I have called you friends."[8] Or again He promises His continual presence, in spite of appearances, to those who have learned His desires. "Where two or three are gathered in My Name, there am I in the midst."[9]…"Behold, I am with you all days."[10] And, as long as you did it to one of these My least brethren, you did it to Me."[11]

If then there is anything clear in the Gospels it is this — that Jesus Christ first and foremost desires our friendship. It is His reproach to the world, not that the Saviour came to the lost, and that the lost ran from Him to lose themselves more deeply, not that the Creator came to the Creature and that the Creature rejected Him; but that the Friend "came unto His own, and that His own received Him not."[12]

Now the consciousness of this friendship of Jesus Christ is the very secret of the Saints. Ordinary men can live ordinary lives, with little or no open defiance of God, from a hundred second-rate motives. We keep the commandments that we may enter into life; we avoid sin that we may escape hell; we fight against worldliness that we may keep the respect of the world. But no man can advance three paces on the road of perfection unless Jesus Christ walks beside him. It is this, then, that gives distinction to the way of the Saint—and that gives

---

[5] Matt. xxvi: 41.
[6] Matt. xxv: 50.
[7] Apoc. iii: 20.
[8] John xv: 15.
[9] Matt. xviii: 20.
[10] Matt. xxviii: 20.
[11] Matt. xxv: 40.
[12] John i: 11.

him his apparent grotesqueness, too—(for what is more grotesque in the eyes of the unimaginative world than the ecstasy of the lover?) Commonsense never yet drove a man mad; it is common-sense that is thought to characterize sanity; and common-sense, therefore, has never scaled mountains, much less has it cast them into the sea. But it is the maddening joy of the conscious companionship of Jesus Christ that has produced the lovers, and therefore the giants, of history. It is the developing friendship of Jesus Christ and the passion that has inspired those lives, which the world in its duller moods calls unnatural, and the Church, in all her moods, supernatural. "This priest," cried St. Teresa, in one of her more confidential moments with her Lord, "this priest is a very proper person to be made *a friend of ours.*"

II. Now it must be remembered that while this friendship between Christ and the soul is, from one point of view, perfectly comparable to friendship between man and man, from another point of view it is incomparable. Certainly it is a friendship between His Soul and ours; but that Soul of His is united to Divinity. A single *individualistic* friendship with Him therefore does not exhaust His capacities. He is Man, but He is not merely A Man: He is The Son, rather than A Son of man. He is the Eternal Word by whom all things were made and are sustained....

He approaches us therefore along countless avenues, although it is the same Figure that advances down each. It is not enough to know Him interiorly only: He must be known (if His relation with us is to be that which He desires) in all those activities and manifestations in which He displays Himself. One who knows Him therefore solely as an Interior Companion and Guide, however dear and adorable, but does not know Him in the Blessed Sacrament—one whose heart burns as he walks with Jesus in the way, but whose eyes are held that he knows Him not in the breaking of Bread, knows but one perfection out of ten thousand. And again, he who calls Him Friend in Communion, but whose devotion is so narrow and restricted that he does not recognize Him in that Mystical Body in which He dwells and speaks on earth—one, in fact, who is a *dévot*, an individualist, and does not therefore understand that corporate Religion which is the very essence of Catholicism; or, again, who knows Him in all these ways, yet does not know Him in His Vicar, or in His Priest, or in His Mother—or, again, who knows Him in all these ways—(who is, in popular language, an "admirable Catholic")—but who does not recognize the right of the sinner to ask for mercy, or the beggar for alms, in His name: or again, who recognizes Him under sensational circumstances, but not under dreary ones—who gives lavishly to the first beggar who pleads in Christ's Name in the street, but fails to find Him in the unappealing dullard—those, in short, who recognize Christ in one or two or three or more aspects, but not in all—(not, at least, in all those of which Christ Himself has explicitly spoken)—can never rise to that height of intimacy and knowledge of that Ideal Friend which He Himself desires, and has declared to be within our power to attain.

Let us then consider the Friendship of Christ under some of these aspects. Truly we cannot live without Him, for He is the Life. It is impossible to come to the Father except by Him who is the Way. It is useless to toil in pursuit of truth, unless we first possess It. Even the most sacred experiences of life are barren unless His Friendship sanctifies them. The holiest love is obscure except it burns in His shadow. The purest affection—that affection that unites my dearest friend to myself—is a counterfeit and an usurper unless I love my friend in Christ—unless He, the Ideal and Absolute Friend, is the personal bond that unites us.

2

THE FRIENDSHIP OF CHRIST

(INTERIOR)

It is not good for man to be alone. —GEN. ii: 18.

IT SEEMS INCONCEIVABLE AT FIRST SIGHT THAT a relationship, which in any real manner can be called a friendship, should be possible between Christ and the soul. Adoration, dependence, obedience, service, and even imitation—all these things are imaginable; but until we remember that Jesus Christ took a human soul like our own—a soul liable to joy and to sorrow, open to the assaults of passion and temptation, a soul that actually did experience heaviness as well as ecstasy—the pains of obscurity as well as the joys of clear vision—until this becomes to us, from a dogmatic fact apprehended by faith, a vital fact perceived by experience, a full realization of His friendship is out of the question.

For just as in the case of ordinary persons the plane of real friendship lies in the communion of the two souls, so it is between Christ and a man. His Soul is the point of contact between His Godhead and our humanity. We receive His Body with our lips; we prostrate our whole being before His Divinity; but we embrace His Soul with ours.

I. Human friendships usually take their rise in some small external detail. We catch a phrase, we hear an inflection of a voice, we notice the look of the eyes, or a movement in walking; and the tiny experience seems to us like an initiation into a new world. We take the little event as a symbol of a universe that lies behind; we think we have detected a soul exactly suited to our own, a temperament which either from its resemblance to our own, or from a harmonious dissimilarity, is precisely fitted to be our companion. Then the process of friendship begins; we exhibit our own characteristics; we examine his: in point after point we find what we expected to find, and we verify our guesses; and he too, no less, follows the same method, until that point is reached (as it is reached in so many cases, though not, thank God! in all), either in a crisis, or after a trying period, when we discover either that we have been mistaken from the beginning, or that we have deceived the other, or that the process has run its course; the summer is come and gone, and that there are no more fruits to gather on either side.

Now the Divine Friendship—the consciousness, that is to say, that Christ desires our love and intimacy, and offers His own in return—usually begins in the same manner. It may be at the reception of some sacrament, such as we have received a thousand times before; or it may be as we kneel before the Crib at Christmas, or follow our Lord along the Way of the Cross. We have done these things or performed those ceremonies dutifully and lovingly again and again; yet on this sudden day a new experience comes to us. We understand, for example, for the first time that the Holy Child is stretching His arms from the straw, not merely to embrace the world—that would be little enough!—but to embrace our own soul in particular. We understand as we watch Jesus, bloodstained and weary, rising from His third fall, that He is asking our own very self in particular to help Him with His burden. The glance of the Divine Eyes meets our own; there passes from Him to us an emotion or a message that we had never before associated with our own relations with Him. The tiny event has happened! He has knocked at our door, and we have opened; He has called and we have answered. Henceforth, we think, He is ours and we are His. Here, at last, we tell ourselves, is the Friend for whom we have been looking so long: here is the Soul that perfectly understands our own; the one Personality which we can safely allow to dominate our own. Jesus Christ has leapt forward two thousand years, and is standing by our side; He has come down from the painting on the wall; He has risen from the straw in the manger—My Beloved is mine and I am His....

II. The Friendship has begun then. Now begins its process.

The essence of a perfect friendship is that each friend reveals himself utterly to the other, flings aside his reserves, and shows himself for what he truly is.

The first step therefore in the Divine Friendship is the revelation by Jesus Christ of Himself. Up to this point in our spiritual life, however conscientious or dutiful that life may have been, there has been a predominant element of unreality. It is true that we have obeyed, that we have striven to avoid sin, that we have received grace, forfeited it and recovered it, that we have acquired merit or lost it, that we have tried to do our duty, endeavoured to aspire and to love. All this is real, before God. But it has not been real to ourselves. We have said prayers? Yes. But we have scarcely prayed. We have meditated—set the points before us, reflected, resolved and concluded; but the watch has been laid open before us to mark our progress, lest we should meditate too long. But after this new and marvellous experience, all is changed. Jesus Christ begins to exhibit to us not merely the perfections of His past, but the glories of His presence. He begins to live before our eyes; He tears from Himself the conventions with which our imaginations have clothed Him; He lives, moves, speaks, acts, turns this way and that before our eyes. He begins to reveal secret after secret hidden in His own Humanity. We have known facts about Him all our life; we have repeated the Catholic creed; we have assimilated all that theology can tell us. Now, however, we pass from knowledge about Him, to knowledge of Him. We begin to understand that Eternal Life begins in this present, for it is to "know Thee, the only true God, and Jesus Christ, whom Thou hast sent."[13] Our God is becoming our Friend.

On the other side He demands from us what He Himself offers. If He strips Himself before our eyes, He claims that we should do the same. As our God He knows every fibre of the being which He has made; as our Saviour He knows every instant in the past in which we have swerved from His obedience: but, as our Friend, He waits for us to tell Him.

It is tolerably true to say that the difference between our behaviour respectively to an acquaintance and to a friend, is that in the first case

---

[13] John vi: 3.

we seek to conceal ourselves, to present an agreeable or a convenient image of our own character, to use language as a disguise, to use conversation as we might use counters; and in the second case that we put aside conventions and makeshifts, and seek to express ourselves as we are, and not as we would have our friend to think us to be.

This then is required of us in the Divine Friendship. Up to now our Lord has been content with very little: He has accepted a tithe of our money, an hour of our time, a few thoughts and a few emotions, paid over to Him in religious intercourse and worship. He has accepted those things instead of ourselves. Henceforth He demands that all such conventions should cease; that we should be entirely open and honest with Him, that we should display ourselves as we really are—that we should lay aside, in a word, all those comparatively harmless make-believes and courtesies, and be utterly real. And it is probably true to say that in practically every instance where a soul believes herself disillusioned or disappointed with the Divine Friendship, it is not that she has actually betrayed her Lord or outraged Him or failed to rise to His demands in other matters; but that she has never truly treated Him as a friend at all; she has not been courageous enough to comply with that absolutely necessary condition of all true friendship, namely, a complete and sincere straightforwardness with Him. It is far less injurious to friendship to say outright, "I cannot do this thing that is asked of me, because I am a coward," than to find excellent reasons for not doing it.

III. Roughly speaking, then, this is the course which the Divine Friendship must take. We must consider later in detail the various events and incidents that characterize it. For it is an immense consolation to remember that there is not one such incident that has not been experienced by other souls before us. The Way of Divine Love has been trodden and retrodden already a thousand times. And it is useful, too, to reflect, before going further, that since this Friendship is one between two human souls, it will follow in a great degree the regular lines of all other friendships.

There are moments in it of bewildering bliss, at communion or in prayer—moments when it appears (as indeed it is) to be the one supreme experience of life; moments when the whole being is shaken and transfused with love, when the Sacred Heart is no longer merely an object for adoration, but a pulsating thing that beats against our own; when the Bridegroom's Arms are about us, and His kiss on our lips....

There are periods too of tranquillity and steady warmth, of an affection at once strong and reasonable, of an esteem and an admiration satisfying to the will and the intellect, as well as to the sensitive or emotional parts of our nature.

And there are periods, too—months or years—of misery and dryness: times at which it seems as if we actually needed patience with our Divine Friend; cases in which He appears to treat us with coldness or disdain. There will actually be moments in which it needs all the loyalty we have not to cast Him off as fickle and deceptive. There will be misunderstandings, darknesses, obscurities.

Yet, as time passes, and as we emerge through these crises one by one, we come more and more to verify that conviction with which we first embraced our Friend. For this is indeed the one Friendship in which final disappointment is impossible; and He the one Friend who cannot fail. This is the one Friendship for whose sake we cannot humiliate ourselves too much, cannot expose ourselves too much, cannot give too intimate confidences or offer too great sacrifices. It is in the cause of this one Friend only and of His Friendship that the words of one of His intimates are completely justified in which he tells us that for His sake it is good to "count all things to be but loss"—"and count them but as dung, that I may gain Christ."[14]

---

[14] Phil. iii: 8.

3

THE PURGATIVE WAY

Wash me yet more from my iniquity.—PSALM l: 4.

THE INITIAL STAGE OF THE FRIENDSHIP formed with Jesus Christ is usually one of extraordinary happiness. For the soul has found for the first time a companion whose sympathy is perfect and whose Presence is continuous. It is not, necessarily, that the soul consciously attends every instant to this new intimate, so much as that she is never wholly unconscious of Him. As she goes about her ordinary business, paying to each detail of it as much attention as ever, the fact that He is present within her is never entirely forgotten: He is there as is the sunlight or the air, illuminating, freshening and inspiring all that she experiences. From time to time she turns to Him with a word or two; at times He speaks gently to her. She views all that she sees from His standpoint, or rather from her standpoint in Him; lovely things are more lovely because of His loveliness; painful things are less distressing because of His consolation. Nothing is indifferent, because He is present. Even when she sleeps, her heart wakes to Him.

Yet this is only the initial stage of the process; and it is sweet largely because it is new. Certainly she has experienced a tremendous fact, yet so far she has but just entered upon it. There outstretches before her a road that ends only in the Beatific Vision; but there are countless stages to be passed before that end is attained.

For the Friendship, as so formed, is not an end in itself. Christ's desire is indeed to consummate it as soon as may be; yet it cannot be consummated by His mere desire. The soul herself must be educated, must be purified and cleansed so perfectly as to be united with Him by nothing except His grace. She must be first purged and then illuminated, first stripped of herself and then adorned with His favours, before she is fit for her final union. These two stages are named by spiritual writers, the Way of Purgation and the Way of Illumination, respectively: and our subject now is the Way of Purgation.

I. At first, as has been said, the soul takes extraordinary pleasure in all those external things which, it appears to her, are sanctified by Christ's Presence, and more especially by those which are most directly connected with His grace. For example, a soul that has just formed this Friendship—that has, perhaps, either just entered the Catholic Church by conversion, or has, for the first time, consciously and deliberately awakened to the glories of Catholicism, or even to some imperfect form of Christianity, as that system through which Christ has approached her—finds an overwhelming joy in even the most exterior details of that system. The human organization of the Church, her methods, her forms of worship, her music and her art—all these things seem to the soul as wholly heavenly and divine.

And, extremely often, the first sign that the Way of Purgation has been really entered, lies in a consciousness that there is beginning for her an experience which the world calls *Disillusionment*. It may come in a dozen different ways.

She may, for example, be brought face to face with some catastrophe in external matters. She may meet with an unworthy priest, a disunited congregation, some scandal in Christian life, in exactly that sphere where Christ seemed to her evidently supreme. She had thought that the Church must be perfect, because it was the Church of Christ, or the priesthood stainless because it was after the Order of Melchisedech; and she finds to her dismay that there is a human side even to those things that are most associated with Divinity on earth. Or it comes to her, perhaps, in forms of worship. The novelty begins to wear off, and the sweetness of familiarity has not yet had time to form; and she finds that those very things which had seemed to her to be the most directly connected with her new Friend are in themselves external, temporary and transitory. Her love for Christ was so great as to have gilded over all those exterior matters which He and she had in common; now the gilding begins to wear thin, and she sees them to be but earthly after all. And, the more acute her imaginative love at the beginning, the more acute her disappointment now.

This then is usually the first stage of *Purgation*; she becomes disillusioned with human things, and finds that however Christian they may be, they are not, after all, Christ.

Immediately the first danger presents itself; for there is no cleansing process which has not within it a certain destructive power; and if she is, after all, but a superficial kind of soul, she will lose her Friendship with Christ (such as it was), together with those little gifts and enticements of His with which He wooed and pleased her. There are wandering souls in the world who have failed under this test; who have mistaken human romance for an internal love, who have turned back again from Christ so soon as He has put off His ornaments. But if she be stronger than this, she will have learned her first lesson—that Divinity is not in these earthly things, that the love of Christ is a deeper thing than the mere presents He makes to His new friends.

II. The next stage of Purgation lies in what may be called, in a sense, the Disillusionment with Divine things. The earthly side has failed her, or rather has fallen off from the reality; now it begins to seem to her as if the Divine side failed her too.

A brilliant phrase of Faber well describes one element in this Disillusionment—the "monotony of Piety." There comes a time sooner or later when not only do the external things of religion—music, art, liturgy—or the external things of earthly life—the companionship of friends, conversation, business relations—things which at the beginning of the Divine Friendship seemed radiant with Christ's love—begin to wear thin; but the very heart and essence of them begin to fail also. For example, the actual exercise of prayer becomes wearisome; the thrill of meditation, so exquisite at first, when every meditation was a looking into the eyes of Jesus, begins to cease its vibrations. The sacraments, which, she has been informed, work *ex opere operato*—(confer solid grace, that is to say, apart from the fervour of the soul's own action)—become wearisome and monotonous, and, so far as she can see, do not fulfil their own promises. The very things that were intended as helps, seem to become additional burdens.

Or she sets her heart, let us say, on some grace or favour, some positive virtue which she *knows* it must be her Friend's will to confer upon her; she prays, she agonizes, she strives, she pleads—and there is no voice nor any that answers. Her temptations are what they have ever been; her human nature, she perceives, after all is unchanged. She had thought that her newly-formed friendship with Christ altered once and for all her old self, together with her relations with him; and, behold! she is the same as ever. Christ has cheated her, it almost seems, with promises He cannot or will not fulfil. Even in those very matters in which she trusted Him most, those very provinces in which He must obviously be supreme, it seems that, after all, He is no more to her than He had been before she knew Him so intimately.

Now this stage is an infinitely more dangerous one than the preceding; for while it is comparatively easy to distinguish between Christ and, let us say, ecclesiastical music, it is not so easy to distinguish between Christ and grace—or rather between Christ and our own imaginative conceptions of what grace should be and do.

There is first the danger of gradually losing hold on religion altogether, during a long lapse of discouragement; of turning with bitter reproaches upon the silent Friend who will not answer. "I trusted You; I believed in You; I thought I had found my Lover at last. And now You too, like all the rest, have failed me." A soul such as this passes often, in a burst of resentment and disappointment, either to some other religion—some modern fad that promises quick and verifiable returns in spiritual things—or to that same state in which she had been before she ever knew Christ. (Only, it must be remembered, a soul that has once known Christ can never be quite as one that has not known Him.) Or there remains one further state more outrageous and unnatural than any—the state of a cynical and "disillusioned" Christian. "Yes, I too," she tells some ardent soul, "I too was once as you are. I too, in my youthful enthusiasm, once thought I had found the secret.... But you will become practical, some day, too. You will understand, too, that romance is not truth. You will become ordinary and workaday like myself....Yes, it is all very mysterious. Perhaps, after all, experience is the only truth worth having."

Yet, if all goes well; if the soul is yet strong enough still to cleave to what seems now a mere memory; if she is confident that an initiation so bewilderingly beautiful as was hers when the Friendship of Christ first came to her, cannot, in the long run, lead to barrenness and cynicism and desolation; if she can but cry in her sincerity that it is better to kneel eternally at the grave of the buried Jesus than to go back and mix again in the ways of the world; then she learns at least one lesson when Jesus rises again (as He always does)—that she cannot hold Him in the old way, because He is "not yet ascended to His Father," and that, in one word, the object of religion is that *the soul should serve God, not that God should serve the soul.*

III. There follows, however, a third stage before the Way of Purgation is wholly passed. The soul has learned that external things are not Christ; that internal things are not Christ. She has become "disillusioned," first with the frame of the picture, and next with the picture itself, before she has reached the original. She now has to learn the last lesson of all, and become disillusioned with herself.

Up to now she has always retained a belief, however faint and humble, that there was something in herself, and of herself, that attracted Christ towards her. She has been at least tempted to think that Christ had failed her; now she has to learn that it is she who, all along, in spite of her childlike love, has been failing Christ; and this is at once the real essence and object of Purgation. She has been stripped of all her coverings, of her ornaments and her clothes; now she has to be stripped of herself, that she may be the kind of disciple that He wishes.

She begins then in this third stage to learn her own ignorance and her own sin, and to learn, too, that which ought to have been wholly incompatible with her ignorance and her sin—her amazing self-centredness and complacency. Up to now she has thought to possess Christ, to hold Him as a lover and a friend, to grasp Him and to keep Him. Her previous mistakes came from this very thing; now she has to learn that not only must she relinquish all that is not Christ, but she *must relinquish Christ*—leave, that is to say, her energetic hold on Him, and be content, instead, to be altogether held and supported by Him. So long as she has a shred of self left she will seek to make the friendship mutual, to give, at least, a fraction of what she receives. Now she faces the fact that Christ must do all, that she can do nothing without Him, that she has no power at all except what He gives her. What has been wrong with her up to now, she begins to see, is not so much that she has done or not done this or that, that she has grasped at this or that… but simply this, that she has been herself all along, that she has sought to possess, not to be possessed…that *she has been herself*, and that that self has been hateful because it has not been altogether lost in Christ. She has been endeavouring to cure the symptoms of her disease, but she has not touched the disease with one finger. *She sees for the first time that there is no good in herself apart from Christ; that He must be all, and she nothing.*

Now if a soul has come so far as this, it is extremely rare that sheer pride should be her ruin. The very knowledge of herself that she has gained is an effectual cure of any further real complacency; for she has seen plainly, at any rate for the time being, how utterly worthless she is. Yet there are other dangers that face her, and of these one at least may be pride under the very subtle disguise of extravagant humility. "Since I am so worthless," she may be tempted to say, "I had better never again attempt those high flights and those aspirations after friendship with my God. Let me give up, once and for all, my dreams of perfection, and my hopes of actual union with my Lord. I must sink back again to the common level, content if I can keep myself just tolerable in His sight. I must take my place again in the ordinary paths, and no longer seek an intimacy with Christ of which I am evidently unworthy."

Or her self-knowledge may take the form of despair; and it is a burden which before now has broken down even the mental faculties themselves. "I have forfeited," cries a soul such as this—a soul which has lost the excuse of pride, but yet clings to its substance—"I have forfeited the Friendship of Christ once and for all. It is impossible that

I who have tasted of the heavenly gift should be renewed again unto repentance. He chose me, and I failed Him. He loved me, and I have loved myself only. Therefore let me go far off from His Presence.... Depart from me; for I am a sinful man, O Lord."[15]

And yet, if the soul only knew it, now is the very moment to which all the preceding stages have led. Now is the very instant in which the beloved soul, having learnt her last lesson of the Purgative Way, is fit to "cast herself into the sea"[16] to come to Jesus. And this she will do, if she has learnt her lesson well, and is conscious that it is exactly because she is nothing in herself, *and because she knows it*, that Christ can be her all, No longer can pride, whether whole or wounded, keep her from Him, for her pride at last is not wounded, but dead....

The way of the spiritual path is strewn with the wrecks of souls that might have been friends of Christ. This one faltered, because Christ put off his ornaments; this one because Christ did not allow her to think that His graces were Himself; a third because wounded pride still writhed, and bade her be true to her own shame rather than to His glory. All these stages and processes are known; every spiritual writer that has ever lived has treated of them over and over again from this standpoint or from that. But the end and lesson of them all is the same—that Christ purges His friends of all that is not of Him; that He leaves them nothing of themselves, in order that He may be wholly theirs; for no soul can learn the strength and the love of God, until she has cast her whole weight upon Him.

---

[15] Luke v: 8.
[16] John xxi: 7.

4

THE ILLUMINATIVE WAY

Thou lightest my lamp, O Lord: O my God, enlighten my darkness.
—PSALM xvii: 29.

IT HAS BEEN SEEN HOW IN THE PURGATIVE WAY, Jesus Christ, in His desire to unite the soul altogether to Himself, strips her gradually of all that would hinder the perfection of that union, and brings her at last to such a "denial" and emptying of self that, seeing her own worthlessness, she casts at last her full weight upon Him who alone can bear it.

But this process is in itself little more than negative. There must follow, if the soul is to make progress, a gradual reclothing of her with the graces in which Christ desires to see her. She has put off the "old man"; she must now put on "the new." To this stage spiritual writers give the name of *Illumination*; and it will be convenient, in treating of it, to follow the same lines as those which have been followed in the treatment of the preceding stage; and to give what may be called specimen examples of the effects of grace, parallel to those by which the Purgative Way has been illustrated.

I. The first stage of the Purgative Way, it has been seen, concerns things external to actual religion: the soul is gradually deepened and sifted by being taught the essential valuelessness both of them and of the emotions which they awaken. The first step of the Illuminative Way, then, may be said to lie, by a paradox, in the instruction which the soul receives as regards their value. (For Grace, it must be remembered, is even more paradoxical than Nature.) In the Purgative Way the soul learns that external things cannot, in themselves, bear her weight—that they are worth nothing. In the Illuminative Way she learns how to use them rightly—that they are worth a great deal.

For example: A soul often complains that she is hindered in her progress by some apparently unnecessary trouble—the constant companionship, let us say, of some person whose temperament jars continually and inevitably with her own. Or it is some untiring temptation from which she cannot escape; some occasion of sin, constantly present, a thorn in the flesh, or a warp in the mind. Or it may be that, by some deprivation, by a bereavement which withdraws all human light and strength from her life, she feels herself maimed and her wings clipped in her struggles upward to God.

Now the most elementary stage in the Illuminative Way consists usually in light gained from our Lord whereby the soul sees the value of those external things. She sees, for instance, that she could never gain supernatural patience or sympathy or largeness of charity, unless there were present always with her some personality which demanded its exercise. Her natural irritation at this unavoidable companionship is a sign that she needs the exercise; and the demand of constant effort at self-control, and finally of actual sympathy, is precisely the means by which she gains the virtue. Or, again, in the case of temptation, there is, humanly, no other way by which certain graces can be assimilated than by their exercise—no other way, for example, by which natural ignorance can be transformed into supernatural innocence; above all, no other way by which the soul can be taught to rely utterly and perseveringly upon God. For it was by some such constant spur as this that St. Paul himself was taught,[17] as he openly confesses, to understand that it is only when human weakness is most sensible of itself that Divine Grace is most effective, or, as he says, "perfected." Finally, by bereavements which seem to shatter the whole life, which leave the weaker character, that has clung to the stronger, helpless and sprawling and wounded—by this means and this means only is the soul taught to adhere utterly to God.

The first step of the Illuminative Way, then, consists, not merely in experiencing these things—for temptations and bereavements are

---

[17] II Cor. xii: 7–9.

common to souls in all stages of the spiritual life—but in perceiving their value, intellectually and interiorly, so clearly and unmistakably that never again, if the soul continues in her course, can she resent or rebel against such things—except perhaps in momentary lapses—but that rather, understanding their value, she bends all her will to accept them and use them as God wills. And it is, therefore, exactly at this stage, that the soul ceases to be bewildered by the Problem of Pain; for, while she cannot, of course, intellectually solve the problem, she answers it, in the only way in which it is possible, by grasping Pain, or at any rate acquiescing in it. She now sees it *practically* to be reasonable; and henceforth endeavours to act upon that intuition.

II. The second step of the Illuminative Way—corresponding to that of the Purgative—consists in light being gained from God as to the reality of interior things—for instance, the truths of religion.

For example: A soul in the elementary stage of faith adheres to an enormous number of dogmas of which she has no interior experience at all. She adheres to them, and lives by them, for the simple fact that she receives them from an Authority which she knows to be Divine. But, not only can she not intellectually understand many of them but she has not what the Scriptures call any "spiritual discernment"[18] with regard to them. She has received the Faith, as our Lord tells us we must all receive it, as a "little child":[19] she holds the casket of the Creed tightly in her hands, guides her life by its light, would die sooner than part with it, and ultimately sanctifies and saves her soul by her simple faithfulness towards it. But she has never dreamed of opening it: or, if she has opened it, all—or at least much—within is dark to her.

Such a soul as this, for instance, wins indulgences by fulfilling the necessary conditions; and can, perhaps, even give the orthodox theological account of what an indulgence actually is; but the spiritual transaction is as impenetrable to her eyes as a jewel in a locked box. Or it may be the doctrine of Eternal Punishment, or the prerogatives of Mary, or the Real Presence. She adheres to these things, and lives

---

[18] John iv: 1; I Cor. xii, etc.
[19] Mark x: 15; Luke xviii: 17.

according to their effects and consequences: but they have no glimmer of light within them so far as she is concerned. She walks wholly by faith, and not at all by verification. She holds the dogmas of faith, but cannot compare them in any sense to natural facts or see those numerous points at which they fit in to other facts of her experience.

But when "Illumination" comes, an extraordinary change takes place. It is not that mysteries cease to be mysteries—not that she can express in exhaustive human language, or even conceive in exhaustive images or modes, those facts of Revelation that are beyond reason—but, for all that, there begins to shine to her spiritual sense, lighted by God's "candle" within her soul, point after point in those jewels of truth which up to now have been opaque and colorless. She can "explain" indulgences, or the justice of Hell, no better than before; and yet there is no longer impenetrable darkness within them. She begins to handle what she has already only touched; to comprehend what she has handled. She finds, by a certain inexplicable process of spiritual verification, that those things which she has taken to be true are *true to her as well as in themselves*; the path where she has walked in darkness, though in security, becomes dimly apparent to her eyes; until, if she, by grace and perseverance, ultimately reaches sanctity itself, she may experience by God's favour those clear-sighted intuitions—or rather that infusion of knowledge—which is so marked a characteristic in the saints.

III. The third stage of Illumination, corresponding with that of the Purgative Way, deals with those actual relations between Christ and the soul that are involved in the Divine Friendship. Now we saw that the last step of the Purgative Way was that abandonment of self into Christ's arms that is only possible when the soul has no longer any self-reliance. The corresponding step of the Illuminative Way is therefore the accession of light which the soul receives as to the abiding Presence of Christ within her, or—perhaps it is safer to say—of her abiding Presence within Christ.

It is at this point, therefore, that the Divine Friendship becomes the object of actual intelligence and contemplation. It is henceforth not only enjoyed, but in a certain degree consciously perceived and understood. This is nothing else than *Ordinary Contemplation.*

Extraordinary Contemplation with its supernatural and miraculous graces and manifestations is a favour bestowed by God *motu proprio.* It is something for which it is practically always presumption to pray—a state which, in its earlier stages, is always to be regarded with self-distrust. This, then, is not our affair at all....But Ordinary Contemplation is not only a state to be prayed for, but a state to which every sincere and devout Christian is bound to aspire, since it is perfectly within his reach by the help of ordinary graces.

It consists in a consciousness of God so effective and so continuous that God is never wholly absent from the thoughts, at least subconsciously. It is a state which, as has been said, the soul, when first initiated into the Friendship of Christ, in the beginning enjoys with extreme though fitful intensity. Life is changed by it: all relations are altered by it; Christ begins to be indeed the Light that irradiates every object of the soul's attention: He becomes the background, or the medium, by whose help all things are seen. Ordinary Contemplation, then, is the fixing of this state by effort as well as by grace. Until the soul has been purged, and until, further, it has been illuminated as to both exterior and interior things, the consciousness of Christ's interior Presence cannot be a continuous state. But when these processes have taken place, when Christ, that is, has trained His new friend in the duties and rewards of the Divine Companionship, Ordinary Contemplation is, if we may say so, the attention that He expects from her. Sin, of course, in this state, becomes subjectively, far more grave: "material" sins easily become "'formal." But, on the other hand, virtue is far easier, since it is difficult for any soul to sin very outrageously so long as she feels the pressure of Christ's hand in hers.

IV. Of course, since every advance in spiritual life has its corresponding dangers—since every step that we rise nearer to God increases the depth of the gulf into which we may fall—a soul that has reached the stage of the Illuminative Way which we have called *Ordinary Contemplation* (and which is, in fact, the point at which the State of Union is reached) has an enormous increase of responsibility. The supreme danger is that of *Individualism*, by which the soul that has climbed up from ordinary pride reaches the zone in which genuine spiritual pride is encountered, and, with spiritual pride, every other form of pride—such as intellectual or emotional pride—which belong to the interior state.

For there is something extraordinarily intoxicating and elevating in the attaining of a point where the soul can say with truth, "Thou lightest my lamp, O Lord."[20] It is bound, in fact, to end in pride unless she can finish the quotation and add, "O my God, enlighten my darkness!" Every heresy and every sect that has ever rent the unity of the Body of Christ has taken its rise primarily in the illuminated soul of this or that chosen Friend of Christ. Practically all the really great heresiarchs have enjoyed a high degree of interior knowledge, or they could have led none of Christ's simple friends astray. What is absolutely needed, then, if illumination is not to end in disunion and destruction, is that, coupled with this increase of interior spiritual life, there should go with it an increase of devotion and submission to the exterior Voice with which God speaks in His Church: for, notoriously, nothing is so difficult to discern as the difference between the inspirations of the Holy Ghost and the aspirations or imaginations of Self.

For non-Catholics it is almost impossible to avoid this elevation of self, this reliance upon interior experience — those elements in fact which still keep Protestantism in being, and still endlessly subdivide its energies: for they are aware of no such Exterior Voice by which their own experiences may be tested. But it is possible, too (as our own days shew), for even educated and intelligent Catholics to suffer from this disease of esotericism, to imagine that the Exterior must be avoided by the Interior, and that they are better able to interpret the Church than is the Church to interpret herself. *Vae soli!* Woe to him that is alone! Woe to him who having received the Friendship of Christ, and its consequent illumination, believes that he enjoys in its

---

[20] Ps. xvii: 29.

interpretation an infallibility which he denies to Christ's outwardly commissioned Vicar!…

For the stronger the interior life and the higher the degree of illumination, the more is the strong hand of the Church needed, and the higher ought to be the soul's appreciation of her office.

It is, we are bound to remind ourselves, from the inner circle of Christ's intimates, from those who know His secrets and have been taught how to find the gate of the Inner Garden where He walks at His ease with His own, that the Judases of history are drawn.

PART II: CHRIST IN THE EXTERIOR

5

CHRIST IN THE EUCHARIST

I am the Bread of Life. —JOHN vi: 35.

UP TO THE PRESENT WE HAVE CONSIDERED the Interior Friendship of Christ with the soul,—a Friendship, it must be remembered, that is open not to Catholics only, but to all who know the Name of Jesus, and indeed, in a sense, to every human being. For our Lord is the "light that enlighteneth every man,"[21] it is His Voice that speaks through conscience, however faulty that instrument may be; it is He, since He is the Only Absolute, who is the dim Ideal Figure discerned standing in the gloom of all hearts who desire Him; it is He whom Marcus Aurelius and Gautama and Confucius and Mahomet, with all their sincere disciples, so far as they were true to themselves, desired, even though they never heard His historical Name of Jesus, or, having heard it, rejected Him, so far as that rejection was without their own fault.

This, then, is the explanation of Non-Catholic, and even of Non-Christian, piety. It would be terrible if it were not so; for in that case we could not claim that our Saviour could be, in any real sense, the Saviour of the world. But that Christ whom we Catholics know to be incarnate and to have lived the Life recorded of Him in the Gospels, has always lived an interior life in the human heart. An old Hindu, it is related, after hearing one sermon on the Life of Christ, begged for baptism. "But how can you ask for it so soon?" inquired the preacher. "Have you ever heard the Name of Jesus before to-day?" "No," said the

---

[21] 1 John i: 9.

old man, "but I have known Him and have been seeking Him all my life long." It was partly in order to convince men of the true nature of sins against conscience—men who "knew not what they did"—that Christ was incarnate and suffered the death of the Cross. "This," He says in effect, "is what you have done to Me interiorly, all your lives."

We pass now to consider another avenue along which Christ approaches us and seeks our friendship; another mode, and, indeed, other gifts which He conveys to us. It is not enough to know Christ in one manner only: we are bound, if we desire to know Him on His own terms and not on ours, to recognize Him under every form which He chooses to use. It is not enough to say, "Interiorly He is my Friend, therefore I need nothing else." It is not loyal friendship to repudiate, for example, the Church or the Sacraments as unnecessary, without first inquiring whether or no He has instituted these things as ways through which He designs to approach us. And, particularly, we must remember, in the Blessed Sacrament He actually conveys to us gifts which we cannot otherwise claim. He brings near to us, and unites to us, not only His Divinity, but that same dear and adorable Human Nature which He assumed on earth for this very purpose.

As we look back over history, the first thought that occurs to us with regard to the Blessed Sacrament is that of the Majesty in which Christ has manifested Himself—how He has used His Sacramental Presence, that is to say, to assert openly and vividly His Royal Sovereignty in this world. Those who have seen earthly monarchs following, bareheaded, Jesus Christ in the Eucharist; those who were present, even in our own day, at those tremendous scenes when, in London, for example, Christ blessed His people from the balcony of the Catholic Cathedral, or in Montreal was lifted up in the open air for the adoration of a hundred thousand persons; those who have ever witnessed, even on the smallest scale, perhaps in some Italian village, a procession of Corpus Christi, have seen the outward emblems not only due to Divinity, but to an earthly sovereignty, openly displayed, cannot help marvelling at the manner in which, under His own guidance, that Sacrament which was instituted under the poorest possible outward conditions, in a mean little upper room, before the eyes of a few uneducated men, has come to be the means by which not only His humility and condescension, but His inherent Majesty, is made visible to the world, whether for that world's adoration or its hostility.

This, however, is not our subject. We are thinking rather of the amazing manner in which Christ in His Sacrament approaches us along our own level of matter and sense; and, in terms that are unmistakable by those who approach Him in simplicity, offers us His Friendship.

I. Explicit devotion to the Dweller in the Tabernacle is, as we know, of comparatively late development. Yet it is a development as inevitably certain, and therefore as Divinely intended, as the earthly splendour which has gradually gathered round that Sacrament, and as the dogmatic conclusions which, though not explicitly worked out in the earliest centuries, are yet irrefutably contained in Christ's own words and were present implicitly to the minds of His earliest friends. In fact in this, as in many other points, the Eucharistic Life of Jesus offers a marvellously suggestive parallel to His Natural Life lived on earth. He who was all Wisdom and all Power "advanced in wisdom and age"[22]—gradually manifested, that is, the characteristics of Divinity—Life and Knowledge—inherently present in His Personality at the beginning. He who worked in the Carpenter's shop was, for all that, God from the beginning. So in His Eucharistic Life. That Sacrament, of which the whole elaborate Catholic doctrine of to-day, has been always true, gradually increased Its own expression, gradually unfolded that which It had always been.

Jesus Christ, then, dwells in our tabernacles to-day as surely as He dwelt in Nazareth, and in the very same Human Nature; and He dwells there, largely, for this very purpose—that He may make Himself accessible to all who know Him interiorly and desire to know Him more perfectly.

It is this Presence which causes that astounding difference of

---

[22] Luke ii: 52.

atmosphere, confessed even by Non-Catholics, between Catholic churches and all others. So marked is this difference that a thousand explanations have to be framed to account for it. It is the suggestiveness of the single point of light burning there! It is the preternatural artistic skill with which the churches are ordered! It is the smell of ancient incense! It is anything and everything except that which we Catholics know it to be—the actual bodily Presence of the Fairest of the children of men, drawing His friends to Himself! Before this strange Presence the bride of yesterday presents the new life now opening before her; the dead man of to-morrow offers the life that is past. The mourners and the happy, the philosopher and the fool, the old man and the child—persons of every temperament, every range of intellect, every nationality—all these unite in that which alone can unite them—the Friendship of the Lover of their souls. Could there be anything more characteristic of the Jesus of the Gospels than this accessibility of His—by which He stands waiting for all who desire to come to Him—this undiscriminating tenderness to those, not one of whom will He cast out? Could there be anything more characteristic of the Christ Who dwells in the heart, than that He Who is so simple interiorly, Who lies patiently within the chamber of the soul, should lie also in the realm without, desiring us to acknowledge Him not only in ourselves, but outside ourselves; not only in interior consciousness, but also, in a sense, in that very realm of space and time which so often seems to obscure His Presence in the world?

It is in this manner, then, that He fulfils that essential of true Friendship, which we call Humility. He places Himself at the mercy of the world whom He desires to win for Himself. He offers Himself there in a poorer disguise even than "in the days of His Flesh,"[23] yet, by the faith and teaching of His Church, by the ceremonies with which she greets His Presence, and by the recognition by His friends, He indicates to those who long to recognize Him and who love Him, and (though they may not know it), that it is He Himself Who is there, the

---

[23] Heb. v: 7.

Desire of all nations and the Lover of every soul.

II. Yet He does not enter the Tabernacle direct. He first becomes present on the altar, at the word of His priest, in the form of a Victim. In the Sacrifice of the Mass He presents Himself before the world, as well as before the eyes of the Eternal Father, in the same significance as that in which He hung upon the Cross, performing the same act which He did once for all, the same act by which He displayed that passion of friendship in whose name He claims our hearts, the climax of that Greatest Love of all by which He "laid down His Life for His friends."[24]

This is, of course, an unthinkable conception to those who know little or nothing of the Living Jesus—whose whole knowledge of Him lies (as they openly admit) within the covers of a printed book. To such as these the Sacrifice is finished and closed in the same manner in which a book itself can be finished, closed and done with—living only, hereafter, in the effect of its energy. Even to those who know more of Jesus than this—who recognize Him as living a real interior life within their own hearts—even to men of real inward spirituality, the doctrine of the continual Sacrifice of the Mass sometimes seems derogatory to the Perfection of Calvary. Yet to the Catholic who enjoys the friendship of Christ, this Sacrifice follows—I might almost say inevitably—from his knowledge of Jesus as "yesterday and to-day and the same for ever."[25] To him, that "finishing" on the Cross is a new beginning. It is that first supreme and inaugural act in which all sacrifices are summed up, and which, in its turn, projects itself into all the future presentations of itself; in such a sense that Christ remains always that which He was on Calvary, the Eternal Victim of this and every altar, through Whom alone we "have access...to the Father."[26]

The Tabernacle, then, presents Christ to us as Friend; the altar presents Him performing before our eyes that eternal act by which He wins in His Humanity the right to demand our friendship.

---

[24] John xv: 13.
[25] Heb. xiii: 8.
[26] Eph. ii: 18.

III. And yet there is one last step of humiliation, even deeper, down which He comes to us—that step by which our Victim and our Friend descends to be our Food. For, so great is His Love to us that it is not enough for Him to remain as an object of adoration, not enough for Him to lie there as our sin-bearer—not enough, above all, for Him to dwell within our souls in an interior friendship in a mode apprehensible only to illuminated eyes. But, in Communion, He hurries down that very stairway of sense up which we so often seek to climb in vain. While we are "yet a great way off"[27] He runs to meet us; and there, flinging aside those poor signs of royalty with which we strive to honour Him, leaving there the embroidery and the flowers and the lights, He not merely unites Himself to us, Soul to soul, in the intimacy of prayer, but Body to body in the sensible form of His Sacramental Life....

This, then, is the last and greatest sign that He could give, in this manner. This is, after all, what Jesus must do. He who sat at meat with the sinners gives Himself to be their meat. He at Whose table we desire to stand as servants comes forth Himself to serve us. He Who lives secretly within the heart, yet Who was Incarnate before men's eyes, once more repeats that crowning act of love and presents Himself under visible appearances to those eyes that desire to see Him. If Humility is the essential of friendship, here, surely, is the Supreme Friend. And those who do not "know Him in the breaking of bread,"[28] however great may be their interior knowledge of Him, cannot know one tithe of His perfections. If He merely lived in Heaven, in His Human Nature at the right hand of the Majesty on high, He would not be the Christ of the Gospels. If He merely lived in His Divine Nature in the hearts of those who received Him and made Him welcome, He would not be the Christ of Capharnaum and Jerusalem. But that He, the Creator of the world, Who made Himself once to be in the form of a creature; that He, Who, dwelling in inaccessible light, descended to our lower darkness—that this God of ours, Who so passionately

---

[27] Luke xv: 20.
[28] Luke xxiv: 35.

desired the friendship of the sons of men as to make Himself in their image and likeness—that Jesus Christ, of the Gospel and the inner life, Who, "rising again from the dead, dieth now no more,"[29] Who has taken up our Human Nature to that glory from which that same Human Nature once brought Him down—that He Who is above all laws should use those laws to His own purposes, and present Himself not once but ten thousand times as our Victim, not once but ten thousand times as our Food, and not once and no more, but eternally and unchangeably, our Friend— this is indeed the Jesus Whom we have known in the Gospels and in our own hearts—our Friend by every right and every claim.

Learn, then, something of His own Humility before the Sacrament which is Himself. As He strips from Himself that glory which is His, we must strip from ourselves the pride to which we have no right—every rag and shred of that complacency and self-centredness that are the greatest of all obstacles to the designs of His Love. We must humble ourselves in the very dust before those Divine and gracious Feet, which, not only in Jerusalem two thousand years ago, but to-day and in these cities in which we live, travel so far to seek and save our souls.

---

[29] Rom. vi: 9.

6

CHRIST IN THE CHURCH

I am the Vine; you the branches. —JOHN xv: 5.

UP TO THE PRESENT WE HAVE BEEN CONSIDERing what may be called the Individual Friendship of Christ for the soul—the relationship with Himself directly, as God dwelling in the heart, as the God-Man in the Blessed Sacrament—that is to say, we have been considering the spiritual life of the individual as developed by the Individual Friendship of her Lord.

I. Now there is scarcely anything so difficult of diagnosis and so easily misunderstood as certain impulses and instincts of the spiritual life. Modern psychologists remind us of what St. Ignatius taught three centuries ago, with regard to the bewildering difficulty of distinguishing the action of that hidden part of our human nature not usually under the direct attention of the consciousness, from the action of God. Impulses and desires rise within the soul, which seem to bear every mark of a Divine origin; it is only when they are obeyed or gratified that we discover that often, after all, they have risen from self—from association, or memory, or education, or even from hidden pride and self-interest—and lead to spiritual disaster. It needs a very pure intention as well as great spiritual discernment always to recognize the Divine Voice; always to penetrate the disguise of one who, in the higher stages of spiritual progress, so often presents himself as an "Angel of Light."

The result is that appalling shipwrecks occasionally occur—or at least lamentable mistakes are made— among souls of whom at any rate it cannot be said that they have not taken great pains with the cultivation of the inner life. There is no obstinacy like religious obstinacy; for the spiritual man encourages himself in his wrong course, by a conviction that he is following Divine guidance. He is not, to his own knowledge, wilful or perverse: on the contrary, he is persuaded that he is an obedient follower of a Divine interior monitor. There is no fanatic so extravagant as a religious fanatic.

It is chiefly, then, from amongst those who have seriously cultivated the inner life that the sharpest criticisms of Catholicism come. Catholics are told that they have substituted a System for a Person; that they are too exterior, too formal, too official. "I possess Jesus Christ in my heart," says such a critic. "What more do I need? I have God within me: why should I go about to seek for a God without me? I know God: does it then matter so much whether I know about Him? Is not a child nearer to his father than a biographer can be? To be 'orthodox' is not so great a matter after all: 'I had sooner love God than discourse learnedly about the Blessed Trinity.'"

The Catholic system, then, is denounced as tyrannical and clumsy. Conscience illuminated by the Presence of Jesus Christ in the heart must be the guide of every man. Any attempt to set up a system, we are told, to lay down limits, any endeavour to guide souls authoritatively, to "bind and loose,"—all these things are a practical denial of the Supreme Authority of Christ within.

What is our answer to this?

Our first observation is the familiar controversial statement— (controversial yet undeniable)—that those Christians who most strongly insist on the sacrosanctity of the inner life, and its sufficiency as a guide, are those who are least able to agree on religious matters. Every new sect that comes into existence in these latter days takes its stand always upon this claim—a claim that has been made incessantly ever since the sixteenth century—yet has never been justified by that unity amongst its supporters which ought, if it were true, to be the result. If Jesus Christ intended to found Christianity upon His own Presence in the heart as a sufficient guide to truth —then Jesus Christ has failed in His Mission.

The next remark that must be made leads to the main subject of our present consideration. It is this, that that very system which is denounced as usurping Christ's Prerogative is a great deal more than a system—that it is in fact, in one sense, actually Jesus Christ Himself, doing that work exteriorly and authoritatively which cannot be done with any certain success in the interior life—subject as that is to a thousand delusions and misunderstandings and complications for which there is no other remedy.

II. It has been pointed out that in the Gospels Christ again and again utters His desire to form a Friendship with souls. It is equally clear in the Gospels that this is not to be merely an interior relation. Certainly He comes to the heart of every man who desires it; but He makes promises that are far more explicit and far-reaching than these, to souls who do not isolate themselves with Him, but unite with other souls. His Presence "where there are two or three gathered together in His Name";[30] His special accessibility to those who "consent upon earth concerning anything whatsoever they shall ask";[31] His promises in fact to guide those who *corporately* seek Him—are indefinitely more emphatic than any pledge He expressly gives to any single soul.

But the affair is much greater than this. For in the words "I am the Vine, you the branches"[32] He actually announces a certain *identity of Himself*—and not merely His Presence—with those who corporately represent Him; and He interprets and formulates all this finally in His tremendous statements: "He that heareth you, heareth Me.[33] ... As the Father hath sent Me, I also send you.[34] ... Whatsoever you shall bind on earth, shall be bound also in heaven.[35] ... Going therefore, *teach* ye all nations.[36] ... I am with you all days."[37]

This, then, is the Catholic position; and it is one not only necessitated by common-sense, but declared by our Lord's own words even more explicitly than is any promise of His to "abide" with the individual. To no single man did Christ ever say explicitly "I am with *thee* always," except, in a sense, to Peter, His Vicar on earth.

Here, then, we have the only possible reconciliation of the fact that

---

[30] Matt. xviii: 20.
[31] Ibid. 19.
[32] John xv: 5.
[33] Luke x: 16.
[34] John xx: 21.
[35] Matt. xvi: 19; xviii:
[36] Matt. xxviii: 19.
[37] Ibid. 20.

Christ is with the soul, and speaks to the soul, and the fact that it is exceedingly difficult for that soul, even in matters of life and death, always to know certainly whether it is the Voice of Christ which speaks, or some merely human, or even diabolical, impulse. According to the Catholic system there is another Presence of Christ, to which the soul also has access, to which He has promised guarantees which He never promised to the individual. In a word, He has promised His Presence upon earth, dwelling in a mystical Society or Body; it is through that Body of Christ that His Voice actually speaks, exteriorly and authoritatively; and it is only by submission to that Voice that we can test these private intimations and ideas, as to whether they are indeed of God or not.

It is obvious, then, that a soul which seeks the Friendship of Christ cannot find it adequately in the interior life only. We have seen how strong and intense this interior life may be; how souls who cultivate it can really and actually enjoy the personal individual Presence of the Divine Friend, even though they may know little or nothing of His action in the world. But how enormous become the possibilities before a humble soul who not only knows Christ in herself, not only studies His character in the Gospel—the written record of His natural life on earth—but has her eyes opened to the astounding fact that Christ still lives and acts and speaks upon earth through the Life of His mystical Body—that the Divine Character sketched in a few lines two thousand years ago is being elaborated and developed through all the ages, under the guidance of His own Personality, in the terms of that Human Nature which He has mystically united to Himself.

The subject is too vast to be spoken of here. Two or three considerations, however, directly concern us.

III. (i) The Catholic soul, considering all this, must develop her Friendship with Christ-in-Catholicism. Indeed, one of the most remarkable facts in the Catholic Religion is the manner in which this is almost instinctively done by persons who perhaps have never deliberately meditated upon the reason of their action. We feel, by a kind of intuition, that the Church is something more than the largest empire on earth—more than the most venerable Society of history; more than the Representative and Vice-regent of God; more even than the "Bride of the Lamb." All these metaphors, however sacred, fall short of the complete Divine reality. *For the Church is Christ Himself.*

Hence a certain "friendliness" with the Church is not difficult. No Catholic, for example, who even attempts to practise his religion, is ever altogether homeless or an exile. He feels, not only as a subject of a kingdom or an empire may feel, protected by his country's flag—but as one who is in the society of a friend. He wanders into churches abroad, not only to visit the Blessed Sacrament, not only to reassure himself as to the hour for mass, but to get into the company of a mysterious and comforting Personality, driven by an instinct he can scarcely explain. He is perfectly reasonable in doing so; for Christ, his Friend, is there, present in that centre of humanity whose members are His.

(ii) But this is not all. In a true friendship between two persons, the weaker of the two must always, little by little, become conformed not only to the habits of life, but to the habits of thought, of the stronger. Little by little the process goes on until that state of mutual understanding is reached which we call "perfect sympathy."

In the interior friendship with Christ this is essential. We must so dwell with Him, as His Apostle tells us, that at last, "bringing into captivity every understanding"[38] to His obedience, we lose, in a certain sense, our own identity. We lose our limited personal way of looking at things, our selfish schemes and ideas, and finally, since our "life is hid with Christ in God,"[39] we no longer live; it is Christ that liveth in us.[40]

Precisely the same thing, therefore, must be aimed at with regard to our friendship with Christ-in-Catholicism.

When a convert begins his Catholic life, or when one who has been a Catholic from the cradle wakes to a deliberate consideration of what his religion means, it is enough to believe all that the Church expressly teaches, and to conform his life to that teaching: just as, in the first

---

[38] II Cor. x: 5.
[39] Col. iii: 3.
[40] Gal. ii: 20.

stage of a new acquaintanceship, it is enough to be polite and deferential and to refrain from offence. But as time goes on, and the relationship deepens, this is not enough. What is courtesy in the first stage, is coolness in the second. As the relationship deepens, it is absolutely necessary, if relations are not to be marred, to begin to conform not only words and actions, but thoughts; and even more than thoughts—instincts and intuitions. Two really intimate friends know—each of them, without a question or word of explanation—what would be the judgment of the other upon a new situation. Each knows the likes and dislikes of the other, even though they may not be expressed in words.

Now this is precisely what a Catholic soul must aim at. If friendship with Christ in the Church is to be real—and without this knowledge of Him, as has been seen, our relations with Him cannot be at all adequately what He intends—it must extend not only to scrupulous external obedience and formulated acts of faith, but to an interior way of looking at things in general; an instinctive attitude; an intuitive atmosphere—such as we see again in simple and faithful Catholics, usually uneducated, who, while knowing little or nothing of exact dogmatic or moral theology, yet detect with an almost miraculous swiftness heretical tendencies or dangerous teaching, which perhaps not even a trained theologian could analyse at once.

There is no more a short cut to this intimate sympathy with Catholicism than to the parallel intimate sympathy with Christ interiorly. Humility, obedience, simplicity—these are the virtues on which the Divine Friendship, as well as mere human friendships, alone can thrive.

And yet, again and again, however well a soul may know all this, she will find herself filled with a kind of repugnance to this attitude which looks so much like servility. "Was I," she will be tempted to ask herself, "was I, after all, only created, and endowed with a temperament and an independent judgment, and personal preferences, and, it may be, the divine gift of originality, merely that I may crush them out, sacrifice them, throw them back, offer them to be reabsorbed in the common stock from which, by my very creation, they were distinguished?"

Ah! Consider it again. Was not your free-will given you that you might, with it, choose to have no will but God's? Your intellect, that it might gradually learn to bring it into obedience with the Divine Wisdom; your heart that it might love and hate those things which the Sacred Heart Itself loves and hates? For in a soul's union with God nothing is lost which she unites with Him. Rather, each gift is transformed, glorified, and lifted to a higher nature. True, she "no longer lives"; but instead it is "Christ that liveth in her."

And if this is true of the soul and God, it is true in whatever form God chooses to present Himself. No higher life can be lived on earth than one of entire and abject imitation of the Life of Jesus Christ: no freedom is so great as that of the children of God who are fast bound by the perfect Law of Love and Liberty.

Once grasp, therefore, that the Catholic Church is Christ's historical expression of Himself: once see in her Eyes the Divine glance, and through her face the Face of Christ Himself: once hear from her lips that Voice that speaks always "as one having authority";[41] and you will understand that no nobler life is possible for a human soul than to "lose herself"[42] in this sense in that glorious Society which is His Body; no greater wisdom than to think with her; no purer love than that which burns in Her Heart who, with Christ as her Soul, is indeed the Saviour of the world.

---

[41] Matt. vii: 29.
[42] Matt. x: 39.

7

CHRIST IN THE PRIEST

Grace and truth came by Jesus Christ. —JOHN i: 17.

IT HAS BEEN SEEN HOW THE CHURCH IS THE Body of Christ, in such a sense that the soul who desires the Friendship of Christ must seek it in the Church as well as in herself—exteriorly as well as interiorly. Certain characteristics of Christ, for example, the knowledge of which is essential to true sympathy with Him—His authoritativeness, His infallibility, His undying energy and the rest—these are appreciated fully only by the fervent Catholic.

Now the Catholic Church is a Society of such vastness, that for the majority of persons it is impossible to form any complete image of her in their minds. Intellectually they know of her; interiorly they bow to her; but, practically, she becomes accessible to them primarily through the priest. This is indeed a common charge brought against the Catholic Church. She exalts, it is said, fallible humanity, in the person of the priest whom not even she believes to be infallible, to heights too giddy to be safe. If it were merely the Ideal Society that was exalted, some excuse could be found; but it is the individual human priest who, as a matter of fact, in the eyes of Catholics parades in the garments of Christ, and is thought to be clothed with His prerogatives. This is largely true. The only possible answer is that Christ did actually intend this to be the case; that He appointed a Priesthood which should not only represent Him and stand for Him, but should *in a certain sense be Himself*—that is to say, that Christ should exercise divine powers through its agency; and that devotion and reverence towards the priest should be a direct homage to the Eternal Priesthood of which the human minister is a partaker. If this is true, it becomes plain that the priest, as well as the Church, is one of those channels through which the devout soul must develop her personal intimacy with her Lord.

I. It is unnecessary to enlarge upon the very evident humanity of the Priest. No priest is mad enough to forget it even for an instant. Even if his personal complacency should blind him to his own defects, society will very soon remind him of it by the examples of others. Again and again, some unhappy priest, seeming to rise step by step in the spiritual life, extending his influence and his reputation, gathering admirers and dependents round him, suddenly offers to the world a heart-breaking reminder of his own weak humanity. It need not be a moral fall—in the narrow sense—thank God! it seldom is that—but how often is there a sudden slackening of zeal, a sudden explosion of ludicrous personal pride, which, in a moment, shakes the souls who have leaned on him, and affords the world one more example of the fact that "Priests are but men after all!" Certainly, priests are but men. Why, then, is the world so shocked to find them men, unless subconsciously at least it is aware that they are a great deal more?

For, first, they are Ambassadors of Christ; and Christ is present in them as a King is present in his accredited Representative. Christ expressly commissions them in this, when He bids His Apostles to go out "into the whole world and preach the gospel to every creature."[43]

This in itself—claimed as it is by every kind of "Christian minister"—involves, by that very fact, an enormous extension of Christ's virtual Presence on earth. "How beautiful," cries the prophet of even the old dispensation, "how beautiful upon the mountains are the feet of him that bringeth good tidings and that preacheth peace";[44] beautiful, since they are feet that carry the love-message of the Fairest of the children of men. Here, then, it is worth while noticing that the priest, so far as he may attempt to be original in the substance of his message, is unfaithful to his commission. Christ does not commission his ambassador to invent treaties of reconciliation, but to deliver the Divine treaty. It is occasionally said that the Catholic Church is the notorious

---

[43] Mark xvi: 15.
[44] Isaias lii: 7.

enemy of thought; that she offers no encouragement, but rather the reverse, to the brilliant explorer in the realms of truth; that she silences or repudiates her ministers the instant they begin to think or speak for themselves. This is exactly true, in the sense that she does not believe that God's Revelation can be improved upon by even the most brilliant human intellect. She does not rebuke those of her ministers who seek originality in the manner of their message, so long as the message is not obscured by their originality; she does not silence those who present old dogmas in new phrases: but emphatically she repudiates those who, as some recent thinkers have attempted to do, seek to present new dogmas under the cover of the old words.

First, then, Christ is in His priest, at least so far as to use his lips for the Divine message. And we may note, in passing, that this requires extraordinary graces in the messenger. There is nothing so irrepressible as human nature; nothing that so yearns to push itself forward; and, simultaneously, nothing in which the human mind takes greater pleasure in speculating and dogmatizing than the region of theology. Yet, in some manner, so overwhelming are the graces with which Christ has strengthened His Church, that it has become a reproach in the world that priests all teach the same dogmas. It is a reproach for which we may thank God.

II. But all this might be done without a *Priesthood* at all. Every non-Catholic minister claims as much. For it is evident that since the Divine Teacher Jesus Christ no longer speaks on earth with His own human lips, He must, so far as the preaching of Revelation is concerned, use other human lips for that purpose. "Truth…came by Jesus Christ";[45] and preaching of that Truth is continued by Him through the mouths of His accredited ministers.

But "Grace" also "came by Jesus Christ."[46] And if the conveyance of Truth by human ministers is not derogatory to the prerogative of Christ as Prophet, it is reasonable to believe that the conveyance of Grace by human ministers is no more derogatory to the prerogative of

---

[45] John i: 17.
[46] Ibid.

Christ as Priest. And this is one essential of the Catholic doctrine of Priesthood.

Christ came to bring life, to sustain it, and to restore it when lost: for He alone, the Prince of Life, possesses the elixir of Life. The Pharisees were right enough, on their premises, in arguing "Who can forgive sins, but God alone?"[47] "How can this man give us His Flesh to eat?"[48] It was the premisses that were wrong; since Christ was more than man. Christ, then, who is the Fountain of Life, alone can give Grace: as Christ, who is the Truth, alone can give Revelation. For Grace is to Life, what Revelation is to Truth. And it is the underlying idea of the Catholic Priesthood, that He commissions and empowers in both departments alike, and not only one, a human ministry to exercise the Divine Prerogatives,

As, therefore, the priest in the pulpit cries, "I say unto you": so in the confessional he whispers "I absolve you," and at the altar "This is my Body."...This, then, is a second, and an overwhelmingly awful thought, yet essential to be understood, if we are to realize in what manner Christ is present in His priest.

First He is present in him when he delivers, it may be more or less mechanically, the message with which he is entrusted. The Divine Prophet uses human lips to "utter knowledge," and to declare truth. But when we reflect that the Divine Priest uses human lips to effect sacerdotal purposes, we see that the Presence is far more intimate than that of a King in his ambassador. For the ambassador is practically *in no sense* His Master: he can dictate the terms of a treaty, but he cannot finally conclude it: he can plead with those to whom he is sent, but he can only in a very limited and representative sense reconcile them to His King. Yet these Ambassadors of Christ, in virtue of the express commission which they have received, in such words as "This is My Body...do this for a commemoration of Me."[49] "Receive ye the Holy

---

[47] Luke v: 21.
[48] John vi: 53.
[49] Luke xxii: 19.

Ghost. Whose sins you shall forgive they are forgiven them"[50]— are empowered to do that which no merely earthly ambassador can do. They effect that which they declare: they administer the mercy which they preach....

Here, then, we can say in reality, that Christ is present in His Priest—present, that is, as He is present in no saint, however holy, and in no angel, however near to the Face of God. It is the priest's supreme privilege, as well as his terrifying responsibility, to be, in those moments during which he exercises his ministry, in a sense Christ Himself. He says not, "May Christ absolve thee"; but "I absolve thee"; not, "This is the Body of Christ"; but, "This is My Body." It is not then merely the utterance of the lips which Christ employs, but Himself for the moment must sway the Will and Intention; since it is a Divine Act that is done. He becomes present in the priest, then, by His priest's permission. As to whether or not, here and now, the Blessed Sacrament is consecrated (that is, the crowning marvel of Christ's mercy consummated)—as to whether, here and now, the sorrowful sinner goes pardoned away—as to whether, in a word, God, in this or that place, at this or that time, *acts as God*—this hangs not merely on the mechanical words uttered by the priest, but by the union of his free-will and free intention with that of his Creator.

III. It seems as if we had wandered far away from our theme—Friendship with Christ. Yet we have never left it for a moment.

We have considered various modes in which Christ's Friendship is made accessible to us; and have seen how it does not consist merely in an interior adherence to Him, but in an exterior recognition and an exterior welcome of Him. His Human Nature comes to us in the Sacrament of the Altar; His Divine authority comes in the Human Nature of those who compose His Church, and have a right to speak in His Name. These various characteristics of His cannot be apprehended—that is to say, Friendship with Him cannot be what He means it to be—without these further modes in which He accomplishes His

---

[50] John xx: 22, 23.

Presence.

And here, in His Priest, is yet another mode.

He dwells here on earth, speaking through the lips of His Priest, so far as that priest utters the authoritative and infallible teaching of the Mystical Body of which he is a mouthpiece. He energizes here on earth, in those Divine acts of the priest which Divine Power alone can accomplish, exercising the prerogative of mercy that belongs to God only, making Himself present in His Human Nature under the forms of the Sacrament which He Himself instituted. And, in addition to all this, He exhibits, in that atmosphere that has grown up about the Priesthood, through the instincts of the faithful rather than through the precise instructions of the Church, attributes of His own Divine character, in sympathy with which consists the friendship of those who love Him. What else is that aloofness and detachment and caste-like spirit so characteristic of the Catholic priesthood, but the aroma of the unapproachable sanctity of God who is Most Holy, on whose Face the angels dare not look—this, translated into terms of common life? What else is the astounding accessibility of the priest to the souls who seek him as priest rather than as man, but the human rendering of the Divine readiness to receive all who are burdened and heavy-laden? The very purity of the priest, his detachment from family ties, his loss as a man of all that normally makes a man—even this is but a far-off glimmer of the radiant Personality of Him who was a Virgin's Son, who chose a Virgin for his forerunner, and a Virgin as His familiar friend—who is followed even among the celestial family of Heaven, "whithersoever He goeth," by men "who were not defiled with women: for they are virgins."[51]

Devotion to the priesthood, then, respect for the office, jealousy for its honour, insistence upon the high standard of those who fulfil it—these are nothing else but manifestations of that Friendship of Christ of which we are treating, and recognitions of Himself in His minister and agent. Not to lean upon the priest— (for no man is capable

---

[51] Apoc. xiv: 4.

of bearing the full weight of another soul)—but to lean indeed upon the priesthood—this is reliance upon Christ: for as you approach the priest, understanding what it is for which you look, and discerning the man from his office, you approach that Eternal Priest who lives in him—Him who is "a priest for ever according to the order of Melchisedech";[52] Him of whom the highest praise which His prophet could utter, was to glorify Him as a "Priest upon His Throne."[53]

---

[52] Ps. cx: 4.
[53] Zach. vi: 13.

8

CHRIST IN THE SAINT

You are the light of the world. —MATT. v: 14.

WE HAVE SEEN HOW CHRIST IS PRESENT IN His Priest through the "character" and the mission that the priest receives. It is Christ who speaks through his mouth when he delivers the message of the Gospel; it is Christ too, who, using the priest's will and intention as well as his words and actions, performs the supernatural acts of the sacramental and sacerdotal rites. Finally, the universal characteristics of the priesthood—such as its separation from the world and, simultaneously, its accessibility—these are nothing else but characteristics of Christ Himself, precipitated, as it were, in a human medium.

But there is another holiness in the world, besides that of external consecration —namely, Personal Holiness or Moral Sanctity. We have now to consider Christ's relations to this also—His Presence in the Saint.

I. When we examine the Catholic religion as it actually surrounds us, we find that the Saints, and, above all, Mary, Queen of Saints, are vital and essential elements in the system. It is certainly true to say that no person born of human parents has exercised and exercises such an influence on the human race as Mary, the Mother of our Lord—or (to put it yet more gently) that no influence is ascribed to any such person as is ascribed to Mary. It is impossible to grasp with the imagination what her Personality has meant to the human race—as is illustrated by the countless services in her honour, the rosaries recited for her intercession and for her praise, the invocations of her name,—in fact, the place she occupies as a whole in the human consciousness. Her name runs through Christian history as inextricably as the Holy Name of

Jesus itself. There is not a circumstance in life, not a situation, not a crisis—we might almost say, not a joy or sorrow—in which, at one time or another, Mary has not been called to take a part. Until three centuries ago her image stood in practically every Christian church throughout the world; at the present day it stands in the vast majority of them, and is slowly re-entering the rest. To the Catholic mind the thought of Mary is united with the thought of Jesus, as inextricably as the two natures in Christ; since, after all, one of those natures comes from her.

We are told, of course, by Protestant critics, that this is exactly where we have erred—that whereas Jesus Christ came to call all men directly to Himself, Mary has been allowed to usurp His place. It is unnecessary to answer this at any length, since every Catholic knows perfectly well that all the worship and honour given to Mary are given with the sole object of uniting the worshipper with that "blessed fruit of her womb,"[54] whom she extends to us in every image, whether as the Child of Joy or as the Man of Sorrows. It is only those who are doubtful, or at least doctrinally vague, as to the absolute Deity of Christ, who can conceive it even as possible for an intelligent Christian to confound Christ with His Mother, or to imagine the Creator and the Creature as standing even in the remotest competition one with the other. As regards the question as to whether we do not learn more of Jesus with Mary than without her, this is exactly the subject under discussion.

First, then, when we turn to the Gospel—that ground-plan of God's designs for mankind—we find that, according to scale, so to speak, Mary occupies a place of dignity beside Jesus wonderfully proportionate to her place in the more explicit Catholic system; since, whenever Her Son comes to a moment of human crisis, whenever a new or startling and fundamental fact is to be revealed concerning Him, Mary is at His side, and is presented, so to speak, in a significant attitude.

---

[54] Luke i: 42.

"The angel Gabriel was sent from God…to a virgin…and the virgin's name was Mary."[55] In such words the first actual step of the Incarnation itself is described, corresponding in an extraordinary manner to that first actual step in the process of the Fall. In both alike we see an Immaculate Maiden, a supernatural messenger, and a choice offered upon which the future shall depend. In the one case Eve's disobedience and love of self was preliminary to the sin by which the race fell; in the other, Mary's obedience and love of God was preliminary to the process by which the same race was redeemed.

Again—as Christ lies in Bethlehem, receiving for the first time as God-made-man the adoration of mankind, it is Mary who kneels beside Him; as Christ through thirty years "learns obedience"[56] as the Son of Man, it is from Mary that He takes His orders. As He steps out into the world to begin that transformation of things common into things divine, it is at Mary's prayer that, in token of His Mission, He turns the water into wine. As He closes His ministry by that yet more amazing miracle to which all other of His signs pointed forward—His own Death upon Calvary—"there stood by the Cross of Jesus His Mother"[57]—as, centuries before, Eve, the mother of the fallen, had stood by that Tree of Death by which the First Adam died. Whether then, we turn to Tradition—that imperishable memory and mind of the Church from which she brings out continually "things new and old"[58]—or to the written record of that Life during which her whole treasure was committed to her care; in either case we find alike that Mary walks always with Jesus—that when we see Him as a new-born Child, we can only find Him "with Mary His Mother";[59] when we adore Him as man, obedient as He would have us obedient, it is in Her house that He lives; when we creep to the Cross to wash ourselves in His Precious Blood, Mary is looking at us from His side. For history too, tells us the same, that where Mary is loved, Jesus is adored; where Mary, the Mother of His Humanity, is despised or slighted, the light of His Divinity goes out….

---

[55] Luke i: 26, 27.
[56] Heb. v: 8.
[57] John xix: 25.
[58] Matt. xiii: 15.
[59] Matt. ii: 11.

II. What is true of Mary is true also of the saints—that wherever Jesus Christ is adored as God, there, like flowers from the earth, His friends spring up in their thousands; that where His Divinity is doubted or denied, the tide of the supernatural sinks with it. And, further, every Catholic knows that the effect of devotion to the saints is devotion to their Divine Lover. Thousands have learned first to know and then to love Jesus Christ, from His intimacy with His dear friends, from their self-sacrifice for His sake, from the manner in which His image has been reproduced in their lives, translated from terms of His Sacred Humanity into terms of their fallen humanity. For how is it possible to make friends with the friends of Christ, without seeking His Divine Friendship also which inspired them?

In what mode, however, is it possible to say that Christ is present in His Mother or in His saints? He is not in them as in the Blessed Eucharist, or as in the Catholic Church, His Body, or as in the priest who supernaturally administers His Eternal Priesthood. They have their lives; He has His. At the utmost is it possible to say more than that they are mirrors of the Divine Light in which we can see His Perfections?

Yet as we look at it, it becomes plain that this is not all; that He is in them as a flame is in a lantern; that their lives are not mere imitations or reflections of His, but actually manifestations of it. The graces that they display are actually the same graces as those with which this Sacred Humanity was saturated; their horror of sin is His; the powers which they exercise are His. They are "the light of the world,"[60] since there burns in them the Supreme Light of the world. Their "life is hid with Christ in God."[61] They have, by the help of grace, hewn at the stone of their human nature, by mortification, by effort, by prayer— even by the final strokes of martyrdom itself—until, little by little, or all at once by sudden heroism, there has emerged from the gross material, not the angel of Michael Angelo, not merely a copy of the Perfect Model; but, in a real sense, that actual Model Himself. It is He Who

---

[60] Matt. v: 14.
[61] Col. iii: 3.

has lived in them, as really, though in another manner, as in the Sacrament of the altar; it is He Who now appears in them in the culmination of their sanctity, visible to all who have eyes to see. Certainly it is not He Himself, pure and simple; since there still remains in every saint that film or glass of his own personal identity which God gave him and can never take away. For it is exactly for the sake of this personal identity, and for the service which it renders to the promulgation of Christ upon earth, that the saint has been created and sanctified. To stare upon the Sun unveiled is to be struck blind, or at least to be so dazzled by excess of light as to see nothing. In the saints, therefore—through their individual characters and temperaments, as through prismatic glass—we see the All-holy Character of Christ, the white brilliancy of His Absolute Perfection, not distorted or diluted, but rather analysed and dissected that we may understand it the better. In the saint of penance it is His sorrow for sin that is made visible; in the martyr His heroic passion for pain; in the doctor of the Church, the treasures of His Wisdom; in the virgin, His purity. In Mary herself the Virgin, the Mother, the Lady of Sorrows, the Cause of our Joy—in Her pierced Heart, in her Magnificat, Her Immaculate Conception—we see, gathered in one individual human person, all the fulness and perfections of all the virtues and graces of which a single soul is capable. "Thou art all fair, O my Love, and there is not a spot in thee."[62]

Here, then, Christ comes to us, extending Himself in that Court of His friends who stand about His Throne. Upon His Right Hand stands the Queen in "gilded clothing," herself a "King's daughter";[63] and on every side, in their orders, those who have learned to call Him Friend, conceived and born in sin, yet who "through many tribulations"[64] have first restored and then retained that image in which they were made, and have so identified themselves with Christ that it is possible to say of them that although they live, it is "now not (they); but Christ that liveth in them."[65]

To seek to separate Christ from His friends, to banish the Queen

---

[62] Cant. of Cants. iv: 7.
[63] Ps. xliv: 10, 14.

Mother from the steps of Her Son's throne, lest she should receive too much love or homage—this is a strange way to seek the Friendship of Him who is their All! A mere individual friendship with Christ in the heart shrinks to a poor isolated thing, thin and loveless (so far as it is possible for one to be loveless, who, however feebly and timorously, seeks the love of Christ), as we see, circle by circle, in the splendour of Catholic faith and practice, new modes radiating out on every side in which we may learn to love our Lord. For He is present in them all, though in each in its own way, as the light of the sun is present in the midday blaze, in the tender lights of dawn, in the pool of water, in the tawny glory of a sunset, in the silver of the moon and the colour of the flower. Once learn that Christ is All, and not merely one among ten thousand—that is, He is *All*— that there is no glory or grace anywhere that is not His, no perfection that is not relative to His Absoluteness, no colour that is not an element of His Whiteness, no sound that is not in the scale of His Music—*once, that is, to rise to what it is that we mean when we name him God*; once escape from that modern spirit of rationalizing away His Deity in the hope of seeing His Humanity; and, behold! we find Him everywhere; we fear nothing except that which separates us from Him, since it is alien to Him—behold! "all things are yours…and you are Christ's: and Christ is God's."[66]

---

[64] Acts xiv: 21; Apoc. vii: 14.
[65] Gal. ii: 20.
[66] I Cor. iii: 22, 23.

9

CHRIST IN THE SINNER

This man receiveth sinners and eateth with them. —*LUKE xv: 2.*

WE HAVE CONSIDERED HOW CHRIST APPROAches us, offering us His Friendship, under various forms and disguises, placing within our reach, that is to say, certain aspects, or even virtues and graces, of Himself which we cannot otherwise apprehend. He extends, for instance, His Priesthood to us in His human priest, and His Holiness in the saint.

Both these particular disguises of His are simple enough. To those who know anything of His Reality as God, it is actually only through some extraordinary prejudice or blindness that they fail to recognize the voice of the Good Shepherd in the words which His priest is authorized to pronounce, or the Sanctity of the Most Holy in the superhuman lives of His closest intimates. It is not so easy to recognize Him in the Sinner; as the Sinner, it would seem, is the one character that He could not possibly assume. Even his dearest disciples seem to have at least been tempted to fail Him when, on the Cross, and yet more in Gethsemane, He "that knew no Sin, for us" was "made sin."[67]

I. First, however, it is clear that among His most marked characteristics, as recorded in the Gospels, were His Friendship for sinners, His extraordinary sympathy for them, and His apparent ease in their company. It was, in fact, for this very thing that fault was found with Him, who claimed, as He did, to teach a doctrine of perfection. And yet, if we think of it, this characteristic of His is one of His supreme credentials for His Divinity; since none but the Highest could condescend so low—none but God would be so human. On the one side

---

[67] II Cor. v: 21.

there is no patronage as from a superior height—"This man receiveth sinners."[68] He is not content to preach to them: He "eateth with them" as if on their level. And, on the other, not a taint of the silly modern pose of unmorality: His final message is always, "Go, and now sin no more."[69]

So emphatic, indeed, is His Friendship for sinners that it seems, superficially, as if comparatively He cared but little for the saints. "I am not come to call the just," He says, "but sinners."[70] Three times over in a single discourse He drives this lesson home to souls that are naturally prejudiced the other way—since the chief danger of religious souls lies in Pharisaism—in three tremendous parables.[71] The piece of silver lost in the house is declared more precious than the nine pieces in the money-box: the single wilful sheep lost in the wilderness more valuable than the ninety-nine in the fold: the rebellious son lost in the world more dear than the elder, and the heir, safe at home.

See, too, how He acted on what He said. It is not merely a vague benevolence that He practises towards sinners in the abstract; but a particular kindness towards sinners in the concrete. He chooses out, it seems, the three types of all sin and unites them in a special manner to His company.

To the careless, reckless, thick-skinned villain He promises Paradise; to the hot-blooded, passionate, sensitive Magdalene He gives absolution and praises her love; and even that sinner most repulsive of all—the deliberate, cold-hearted traitor who prefers thirty shillings to His Master— He greets even in the very moment and climax of his treachery with the tenderest title of all—"*Friend*," says Jesus Christ, "whereto art thou come?"[72]

One lesson emerges, then from the Gospel story clearly enough. We cannot know Christ in His most characteristic aspect until we find Him among the Sinners.

II. What, however, does this mean? Again and again the world

---

[68] Luke xv: 2.
[69] John viii: 11.
[70] Matt. ix: 13.
[71] Luke xv.
[72] Matt. xxvi: 50.

revolts. We can recognize our Priest when he ministers at His altar; our King of Saints when He is transfigured; we can even recognize Him, in a manner, ministering to sinners—since He ministers to ourselves—but is there any intelligible sense in which we can say that He identifies Himself with them, in such a sense that we are to seek Him *in* them, and not merely amongst them?

Yet the example of the saints is clear and unmistakable. Souls that are wholly united to Christ seek nothing except Christ; and, if one thing is plain, it is that such souls, whether they retire from the world to labour in penance and prayer or plunge into the world in effort and activity, are seeking not merely things alien to Christ that they may make them His, but Christ Himself, in a sense, alien to Himself, that they may reconcile them....

After all it is very simple; since Christ is the "Light which enlighteneth every man coming into this world,"[73] and it is the Presence of Christ, and that only, that makes a human soul of any value. Certainly in one sense, the soul lost in sin has lost Christ—His Presence is no longer in the soul by grace; yet in another sense, and an appallingly real and tragic one, Christ is there still. If a sinner merely drove Christ away by his sin, we could let such a soul go; it is because, in St. Paul's terrifying phrase, the sinful soul holds Christ still, "crucifying" Him and "making Him a mockery,"[74] that we cannot bear to leave him to himself. Such a soul has not yet entered Hell; nor yet lost, finally and eternally, the Presence of God; she is still in a state of probation, and therefore still holds her Saviour in mystical bonds and fetters. There, then, our Friend is not merely pleading with the soul externally, but, in a manner, internally too: there in the half-stifled voice of conscience is the Voice of Jesus Christ entreating through lips bruised once again. There lies the Light of the World, crushed to a glimmering spark by a weight of ashes; the Absolute Truth, half-silenced by Falsehood; the Life of the World to come pressed to the brink of death by a life still in this world, and of it.

---

[73] John i: 9.
[74] Heb. vi: 6.

From such a soul, therefore, our Lover cries with the bitterest pathos of all—"Have mercy on me, O my friends.... In the words of my priest I can still perform actions of wonder and mercy; in the lives of my Saints I can live again a holy life on earth; by every soul in grace I am at least tolerated and left in peace, if not actually welcomed. But in the soul of this sinner I am powerless. I speak, but I am not heard; I struggle and am struck down.... 'Attend, and see if there be any sorrow like to my sorrow'.[75]... Behold, 'I thirst'[76]..."

There then is Christ, in the disguise of one who has rejected Him.

III. Now this recognition of Christ in the Sinner is the single essential to our capacity for helping the sinner. We must believe in his possibilities. And his only "possibility" is Christ. We have to recognize, that is to say, that beneath his apparent absence of faith there is still, at any rate, a spark of hope; beneath his hopelessness, at least a glimmer of charity. Mere pleading and rebuke are worse than useless. We have to do, on the level of our own capacities, something of what Christ did in His Omnipotent love—identify ourselves with the sinner, penetrate through his lovelessness and his darkness down to the love and light of Christ Who has not yet wholly left him to himself. We have, in a word, to make the best of him and not the worst (as our Lord does for ourselves every time He forgives us our sins), to forgive his trespasses as we hope that God will forgive our own. To recognize Christ in the sinner is not only to Christ's service, but to the sinner's as well.

Yet how pitiable is the failure of Christians to understand this—or, at any rate, to act upon it! It is easy enough to persuade men to take part, let us say, in a liturgical function where Christ is evidently honoured; to adore Him in the Blessed Sacrament; to reverence Him in His priests; to celebrate the feast of a saint. But it is terribly difficult to persuade them to engage in work whose material lies in Christ's dishonour—to support, let us say, Rescue Societies, or guilds for the conversion of the heathen. We are terribly apt to hug ourselves in our own religion, to leave sinners to themselves, to draw the curtains close,

---

[75] Lam. i: 12
[76] John xix: 28.

to make small cynical remarks, and to forget that a failure to recognize the claim of the heathen and the publican is a failure to recognize the Lord whom we profess to serve, under the disguise in which He most urgently desires our friendship.

Look at the crucifix. Then turn and look at the Sinner. Both are, in themselves, repulsive and horrible to the eyes of cold and godless perfection: both are lovely and desirable, since Christ is in both: both are infinitely pathetic and appealing, since in both He "that knew no sin" is "made sin."[77]…For the crucifix and the Sinner are profoundly, and not merely superficially, alike in this—that both are what the rebellious self-will of man has made of the Image of God; and therefore should be the object of the deepest devotion of all who desire to see that Image restored again to glory—of all who pretend even to any sympathy with Him who not only is the Friend of Sinners, but chooses to identify Himself with them.

To fail to recognize Christ, therefore, in the sinner is to fail to recognize Christ when He is most fully and characteristically Himself. All the devotion in the world to the White Host in the monstrance; all the adoration in the world to the Stainless Child in the arms of His Stainless Mother—all this fails utterly to attain to its true end, unless there accompanies it a passion for the souls of those who dishonour Him, since, beneath all the filth and the corruption of their sins, He who is in the Blessed Sacrament and the Crib dwells here also, and cries to us for help.

Lastly, it is necessary to remember that if we are to have pity on Christ in the Sinner, we must therefore have pity on Christ in ourself.…

---

[77] II Cor. v: 21.

10

CHRIST IN THE AVERAGE MAN

As long as you did it to one of these my least brethren, you did it to me.
—MATT. xxv: 40.

WE HAVE SEEN THAT IT IS COMPARATIVELY easy to recognize Christ in the Priest and the Saint. In the Priest He sacrifices; in the Saint He is transfigured—or, rather, transfigures humanity once more with His own glory. And the only difficulty in recognizing Christ in the Sinner is the same as that which makes it hard to see Him in the Crucifix—a difficulty which, when once surmounted, becomes luminous with the light which it sheds upon the Divine Character. We have seen, too, that those who do not see Christ in these types of humanity lose incalculable opportunities of approaching Him and of apprehending the fullness and variety of that Friendship which He extends to us.

But Christ has even more strange disguises than any of these; and that which is perhaps more strange than all is that which He indicates to us when He tells us that not merely this or that man in particular, but the "average man"—our "neighbour"—is His representative and Vicar on earth as fully (though in wholly another sense) as Priest or Pontiff.

I. He reveals this fact to us in the parable in which He describes His own return to judge mankind.[78] On the one hand, He tells us, stand the saved; and on the other the lost; and the only reason He actually assigns, in this particular discourse, for that eternal separation between the two companies, is that those in the first have ministered to Him in their neighbour; and those in the second failed so to

---

[78] Matt. xxv: 31 ff.

minister. "As long as you did it, or did it not, to one of these my least brethren, you did it, or did it not, to me." These then enter into life; and those into death.

Immediately we are puzzled by the apparent ignorance—it would seem genuine and sincere ignorance—of both one class and the other as to the merit or demerit of their lives. Both alike deprecate the sentence of acquittal and condemnation respectively: "Lord, when did we see thee hungry,...or thirsty,...or naked...or sick or in prison?"..."We have never knowingly served Thee," say the one. "We have never knowingly neglected Thee," say the other. In answer our Lord repeats the fact that in serving or neglecting their neighbours, they have, respectively, served or neglected Himself. Yet He does not explain how actions done in ignorance can either merit or demerit in His sight.

But the explanation is not so difficult. It is that the ignorance is not complete. For it is an universal fact of experience that we all feel an instinctive drawing towards our neighbour which we cannot reject without a sense of moral guilt. It may be that owing to ignorance or wilful rejection of light a man may fail to understand or believe the Fatherhood of God and the claims of Jesus Christ; it may even be that he sincerely believes himself justified intellectually in explicitly denying those truths; but no man ever yet has lived a wholly selfish life from the beginning, no man has ever yet deliberately refused to love his neighbour or to deny the Brotherhood of man, without a consciousness, at some period at least, that he is outraging his highest instincts. Christians know that the Second Great Commandment draws its force only from the First; yet, as a matter of fact, in spite of this, it is perfectly certain that though some men fail, for one reason or another, to feel the force of the First, no man has ever yet, without a sense of guilt, totally rejected the Second.

For Christ is the Light that enlightens every man.[79] It is actually the Voice of the Eternal Word, although His Name and His historical actions may be unknown, that pleads in the voice of conscience.

---

[79] John i: 9.

In rejecting, therefore, the claims of his neighbour, a man is rejecting the claims of the Son of Man. It is no excuse to plead ignorance as to the fact that the historical figure of Christ demands our worship; that is not the point. It remains true that to neglect one's neighbour is to reject an interior impulse, imperious and judicial, which, in spite of the man's ignorance as to its origin and as to its identity with the Voice that spoke in Judea, for all that has a claim upon his sense of moral right. Pilate was not condemned for not knowing the articles of the Nicene Creed, and for not identifying the Prisoner brought before him: he was condemned because he rejected the claims of justice and of the right of an innocent man to be acquitted. He outraged Incarnate Truth because he outraged Justice.

Here then is an undeniable fact. The man who does not keep the Second Commandment cannot even implicitly be keeping the First: the man who rejects Christ in man cannot accept Christ in God. "He that loveth not his brother whom he seeth, how can he love God, whom he seeth not?"[80]

II. Now we have considered how comparatively easy it is to recognize Christ under what we may call His more sensational aspects. The very wondering admiration that we feel at the superhuman exploits of the saints; the shuddering repulsion of which we are conscious in face of the inhuman degradation of the more appalling kinds of sinners—these are, at the least, an unconscious homage on our part to the divine image and Presence within them, manifested by the first and outraged by the second. It is not so easy, however, to recognize Christ in the average man—any more than it is easy to recognize the Divine will and guidance in humdrum circumstances. How, we ask ourselves, is it possible for the Unique to disguise Himself under the Ordinary, for the Fairest of the children of men to hide Himself under the merely unattractive, for the One "chosen out of thousands"[81] to be concealed beneath the Average? Yet, if the love of our neighbour means anything, it means exactly this. "Christ in the heart of every man who thinks

---

[80] I John iv: 20.
[81] Cant. v: 10.

of me"…(as well as in the heart of every man who never gives me a thought). "Christ in the mouth of every man who speaks to me. Christ in every eye that sees me. Christ in every ear that hears me."[82] The husband, for example, has to see Christ in the frivolous wife who spends half her fortune and all her energies in the emptiest social ambition. The wife has to see Christ in the husband who has no idea in the world beyond his business on weekdays and his recreation on Sunday. The middle-aged woman living at home has to find Christ in her garrulous parents and her domestic duties: and her parents have to find Christ in their unimaginative and unattractive daughter. The Benedictine has to see in every guest that comes to the monastery no one less than his own adorable Lord and Master. In our neighbour, that is to say, and in the average plane in which he and we move—"in the fort, in the chariot-seat, in the ship"[83]—we have to find Him Who inhabits eternity; or we cannot claim to know Him as He is.

III. To do this perfectly and consistently is Sanctity. To find Him here is to find Him everywhere. If we find Him here, how much more easily shall we find Him in the Saint, the Sinner, the Priest, the Church and the Blessed Sacrament. And there is no short cut to Sanctity.

Two considerations, however, are worth remarking:

(1) We have to remind ourselves constantly of the duty, and to remain discontented with ourselves until we are at least attempting to practise it.

For the very charms and allurements of what is usually known as "religion" have this extraordinary danger attached to them—that we should mistake them for religion itself. Hardly any danger is so great as this, in these times of ours when religion calls to its aid so many beauties of art and devotion. We may go even further, and say that actual God-given consolations, given "for our health," may "become to us an occasion of falling." Christ caresses the soul, entices it and enchants it, especially in the earlier stages of the spiritual life, in order to encourage it to further efforts; and it is, therefore, a very real spiritual snare

---

[82] The "Breastplate of St. Patrick."
[83] Ibid.

that we should mistake Christ's gifts for Christ, religiosity for religion, and the joys possible on earth for the joys awaiting us in heaven—in a word, that we should mistake the saying of "Lord! Lord!" for the "doing the Will of the Father who is in heaven."[84] Continually and persistently, therefore, we have to test our progress by practical results. I find it easier and easier to worship Christ in the Tabernacle: do I therefore find it easier and easier to serve Christ in my neighbour? For, if not, I am making no real progress at all. I am not advancing, that is to say, along the whole line: I am pushing forward one department of my life to the expense of the rest: I am not developing my Friendship with Christ: I am developing, rather, my own conception of His Friendship (which is a totally different thing). I am falling into the most fatal of all interior snares.

"I find Him in the shining of the stars.
I find Him in the flowering of the fields.
But in His ways with man I find Him not."[85]

And therefore I am not finding Him as He desires to be found.

(2) A second aid to this recognition of Christ lies in an increase of self-knowledge. My supreme difficulty is the merely superficial and imaginative difficulty of realizing how it is possible to discern the Unique beneath the disguise of the Average. Therefore, as I learn to know myself better, and learn therefore how very average I myself am, and, at the same time, discover that Christ still bears with me, tolerates me and dwells within me, it becomes easier for me to realize that Christ is also in my neighbour. As I penetrate deeper and deeper by self-knowledge into the strata of my own character, learning afresh with each discovery how self-love permeates the whole, how little zeal there is for God's glory, and what an immensity of zeal for my own, how my best actions are poisoned by the worst motives—and yet, all through, that Christ still condescends to tabernacle beneath it all and to shine in a heart so cloudy as mine—it becomes increasingly easy for me to understand that He can with even greater facility lie hid be-

---

[84] Matt. vii: 21.
[85] *Morte d'Arthur*, Tennyson.

neath that exterior of my neighbour whom I find so antipathetic, but of whose unworthiness I can never be so certain as I am of my own.

"Cleave the Wood"—look down into your own wooden stupidity of head, "and you shall find me. Lift the stone"—wrench out that rocky senseless thing that you call your heart "and I am there."[86] And then, having found Christ in yourself, go out and find Him in your neighbour too.

---

[86] From the "Logia of Jesus."

11

CHRIST IN THE SUFFERER

I fill up those things that are wanting of the sufferings of Christ. —Coloss. i: 24.

WE HAVE CONSIDERED HOW CHRIST, THE Key of the House of David, is the solution and answer of many doctrines found difficult of apprehension by Non-Catholics. For example, we are thought to "preach the Church rather than Christ," to be superstitious, if not idolatrous, in our worship of the Blessed Sacrament or in our reverence for the Saints, to exalt overmuch the Christian priesthood, to be too friendly towards sinners and too easy in our absolutions. And it is not until the mind grasps that Christ is the solution of each, that the difficulty vanishes in a blaze of light: for, so soon as it perceives that the Church is the Body in which Christ dwells and energizes, that the Blessed Sacrament is Himself in the very Human Nature in which He lived on earth and now triumphs in Heaven, that the sanctity of the Saints is His own, that sacerdotal words and actions are the words and actions of the Eternal Priest, and that the supreme claim of sinners or other persons lies in the Presence of Christ outraged and crucified or neglected within them—the instant these things are seen, and Christ is perceived as extended within these planes and realms, in each in its own manner and degree, not only do difficulties vanish, but new and astounding avenues are opened up by which Christ can be approached and apprehended as the Lover and Friend of Souls, desirous only to be known and loved.

Let us consider one more such type—a problem indeed that stretches wider than dogmatic Catholicism, since it is present in every philosophy and every religion—and see whether Christ is not the Key of this also—the Problem of Pain.

I. It is this problem that stands in the heart of every attempt to solve the riddle of the Universe—the question as to why pain is, or seems to be, the inseparable accompaniment of life. A thousand attempts have been made to answer it. One answer is that of Monism—that there is in existence no actual God at all of infinite Love and Power, and that pain is merely another name for the upward effort of the inchoate Divinity to realize Itself. Another answer is that of the Buddhist—that pain is the inevitable consequence of personal sin, and that the sufferings of each individual are the punishment of his guilt in a previous life. It has been reserved for a sect of our own days to maintain that there is no problem, because there is no pain!—that the whole thing is an illusion; that "thinking makes it so." But no attempt is made in this system to explain why thinking should take this unhappy form, nor why we should think so at all.

Here then the problem stands. We see it, crying for a solution in every innocent child that suffers in his body, it may be, for the sins of his parents; in every anxious heart tormented by sympathy or by the result of crimes for which it is not responsible; and, above all, in every burdened and darkened soul that believes that she has mortally and irreparably offended a God whom she has always striven to serve. It is not the direct and evident consequence of personal sin to the sinner which we find difficult; we are not shocked when the murderer is hanged or the wife-beater flogged—so far, our ideas of justice and the Divine Idea run in agreement. But it is when, let us say, a child who is incapable of learning a moral lesson, suffers for a sin which he cannot even understand; or when a naturally sweet character is, apparently, maddened and embittered by a pain which he cannot see that he has deserved—when sorrow is borne, over and over again, by souls who seem to have a claim on joy, while on the other hand we see "the wicked also highly exalted"[87]—it is then that we are bewildered.

II. First, it is necessary to remark that the chief reason why the intellect fails always to analyse satisfactorily this supreme problem, is because it was never intended to do so. It would be as foolish to attempt to put a mother's love under a microscope, or to "search the universe with a telescope" in the hope of finding God. For pain is one of those vast fundamental facts that must be scrutinized by the whole of man—his heart and his will and his experience—as well as by his head; or not at all. Strictly speaking the intellect is only adequate to the "exact sciences," which is another name for intellectual abstractions from the realm of concrete fact. I can add two and two together infallibly, because "two and two" is an abstraction which my intellect makes from the world around me. But I cannot place two persons together and calculate exactly the effect upon their future lives, or, it may be, upon myself. If the Problem of Pain is to be solved at all, it must be solved by man, not by a part of him.

And when we turn to Christ crucified, knowing who and what He is, we see the problem set before us in its most acute form. It is not a man who hangs there, however innocent; it is Man without his guilt. And it is not merely unfallen Man who hangs there, it is Incarnate God. Certainly this does not answer the problem as to how it can be just that one can suffer for the sins of another; but it does unmistakably shew to us that one can so suffer, conscious of the fact, and can acquiesce in it; and, further, that this Law of Atonement is of so vast and fundamental a sweep and effect that the Lawgiver Himself can submit to it. It gives us then, as Christians, exactly the reassurance that we need; since it is demonstrated to us that pain is not an unhappy accident of life, not a piece of heartless carelessness, not a labouring struggle upwards on the part of an embryo God; but a part of life so august and so far-reaching that, since the Creator Himself can submit

---

[87] Ps. xxxvi: 35.

to it, it must fall under that Divine standard of Justice into which our own ideas of justice must some day be expanded. This does not explain the problem; it makes the steps of its working out even, perhaps, more bewildering than before; yet for Christians it does this at least—it demonstrates the total sum worked out and "placarded"[88] (in St. Paul's phrase) before our eyes.

Accepting this, then, so far as a working hypothesis—so far as to believe that the Atonement that Christ wrought is according to this incomprehensible law—we turn again to those other innocent sufferers—to the crippled child, the agonized mother, the darkened melancholic soul.

Now if we isolate these sufferers from the rest of the human race, it we take them out of their context and regard them one by one, again we are baffled. But if, on the other hand, we do that which we have been doing throughout these considerations—meditate, that is, upon how it may be possible to see Christ in them—light begins to glimmer at once....

We reflected not long ago on the claim of the Church—the sanctified organ of humanity—to be the body in which Christ dwells. So far as this is so, then, we see, as in the authority of the Church the authority of Christ, His sanctity in hers, His priesthood in her ministers, so in her pains His Calvary. These sufferers, then, are extensions of Himself crucified, as His priests are His agents. That which He did on Calvary—that mysterious atonement in which Humanity united to God was the victim—He represents, as we have seen, in the Sacrifice of the Mass; now we see again how He offers once more that same sacrifice, though in another mode altogether, under the terms of the blood and tears of those who are united with Him. "I fill up," says St. Paul, "those things that are wanting of the sufferings of Christ."[89] "I work out, that is," the sufferer may say, "under terms of my own humanity, that atone-

---

[88] προεγράφη, Gal. iii: 1.
[89] Col. 1: 24.

of human decency and gratitude and justice; they knew, like Pilate, that they were killing a just man, that they were taking upon their own heads the blood of an innocent person. But they did not know that they were crucifying the Lord of Glory, that they were attempting to silence the Eternal Word.

This, then, can at least be said in their favour—"They know the horror, but not the full horror, of what they do. Therefore, Father, forgive them."

II. "As it was in the beginning, is now and ever shall be." The world, as well as Jesus Christ, is the same yesterday, to-day and for ever. There is a Society in the world in which Jesus Christ dwells perpetually; and this Society, like Jesus Christ, is at once Divine and human. This Society, then, the Catholic Church, is ceaselessly engaged in both Divine and human works; and, like Jesus Christ Himself (and like every activity for good), meets with amazing ingratitude. Once more in our own day—as in England three centuries ago, in Rome sixteen centuries ago—this Society is in the act of being crucified by those whose relief and salvation it is her one desire to bring about. It is, in fact, a condition of things which must be perpetual so long as the world remains what it is; though this period or that may exhibit the fact more startlingly.

It is impossible to say that men do not know, at least in part, what it is that they do. They know that the whole of European civilization rests upon Catholic foundations—that the Church fed the hungry, taught the ignorant, befriended the outcast, and made life tolerable to the sufferers, centuries before the State dreamed of doing so, before, indeed, there was anything that could be called a State, to do so. They know that she has been the mother of ideals, of the noblest art and the purest beauty. They use to-day, in every country of Europe, for secular or semi-sacred purposes, buildings which she raised for her own worship of her God. They know that the morals of men find their only ultimate sanction in her teaching—that where dogma goes down, crime goes up. And here, again, the only charge against her is that she is no friend to Caesar—no friend, that is, to any system that seeks to organize society apart from God.

But, thank God! Divine Charity can still plead for men that they do not know the full horror of what they do, that they still think that to cripple and torture the Church of God is to do God service. For they do not know that she is His Darling, and the Bride of His Son; that she is the Eternal City coming down from God out of heaven; that, further, in these very sufferings of hers, she is accomplishing and applying Divine Atonement for the sins of those who crucify her.

They know that they are outraging human justice, that they are dealing with a world-wide community in a manner in which they dare not deal with any nation; that they are severing the branch which supports themselves. But they do not know that in this instance human justice is a Divine Right; that in this instance a Society is a Body which incorporates, not the lives of men, but the Incarnate Life of God; that they are slaying, not a Prophet or a Servant, but an Only-Begotten Son.

This prayer, then, is one which we can take upon our own lips.... We have abused the French Republic and the Portuguese revolutionists, and the Italian Freemasons, and the Spanish anarchists, and the Irish Orangemen long enough. In the very point of our agony we must learn to pray. Forgive them, for they know not what they do.

III. Lastly, it is for ourselves also that Jesus prays: since we too, in our own measure, have sinned in frantic ignorance.

For here are we Catholics to whom have been committed the treasures of truth and grace; and here about us is the world to whom we have not transmitted them. We confess to a little sloth and lethargy, a little avarice, a little lack of generosity. We "know what we do," in part: we know we are not faithful to our highest inspirations, that we have not done all that we might, that we have shown a little self-will, a little malice, a little pardonable temper. And we confess these things, and give an easy absolution. And yet we know not what we do. We do not know how urgent is the need of God, how tremendous are the issues He has committed to our care, how enormous is the value of every soul—of every act and word and thought that help to shape the ment which He offered in His own. I am the minister of Christ, as His priest in one manner, His Saint in another, and his whole Church in a third." It does not greatly affect the situation whether or no the sufferer may be fully or indeed at all conscious of his work, for it is in virtue of the humanity common to himself and Christ that his pain avails; the priest at the altar may be an infidel, or violently distracted, yet he consecrates the Body of the Lord; the fever-patient may be rebellious and break out into furious complaint, yet it is nevertheless the patient Christ who suffers in him.

What, then, is the value of a willing sacrifice? It lies in this at least, that it solves practically and satisfactorily the whole problem of pain; since the words a *willing sufferer* are merely a phrase to describe a soul who has solved it—not, that is to say, that he has done the impossible and compressed the problem into the limits of his own intellect, but that he has, somehow or another, succeeded in doing that which the intellect alone could not enable him to do—he has risen with his whole being (worked upon by that Divinity of which the Law of Atonement is an evident principle), has risen to that high atmosphere in which Christ rendered His Soul into His Father's hands, and embraced, and thereby silenced for ever, at least in himself, that question which tortures perpetually those of us who merely stand by and look on.

III. How august and tremendous, therefore, becomes the dignity of the suffering soul, who, seeing Christ within her, desires to unite her pain with His, or, rather, to offer her pain as the instrument of His atonement, since Christ alone can bear the sins of the world! These living crucifixes stand clear altogether of that wrangling world of controversy in which we ourselves dispute. And we, too, looking upon them and seeing in them not merely separate human souls that twist in agony, but souls in whom Christ is set forth evidently crucified, learn one more lesson of the Friendship of Christ—the last, perhaps, to be learned of all—that He who in His glorious and mystical Body demands our obedience, in His Sacramental Body our adoration, in His

Priest our reverence, in His Saints our admiration, and for His dear sinners our forgiveness, asks too, in those who are conformed to Him outwardly as well as inwardly—who bear their pain solely because He bears it for them—for that which is the most sweet of all the emotions that go to make up friendship,—our tenderness and our compassion.

"I fill up those things that are wanting of the sufferings of Christ."[90]

Then let us make haste to minister wine at last, instead of vinegar to our Friend who cries for it.

---

[90] Col. i: 24.

PART III: CHRIST IN HIS HISTORICAL LIFE

12

THE SEVEN WORDS

Christ our Friend Crucified

I

WE HAVE BEEN CONSIDERING SO FAR THE Friendship of Jesus Christ, and the various modes in which He offers it to us, whether interiorly or exteriorly, in the depths of our own consciousness, or in His representatives on earth, each in his various degree. To-day we turn back to the Gospels for the actual record of that supreme pledge of friendship which He gave once for all, the manifestation of that greatest of all Loves by which He laid down His Life for His friends. As we look on Him crucified, we see a bewildering wealth of functions which He performs for us on the Cross; like a Sovereign He bears upon His own wounded Breast all those orders and insignia, which He alone can bestow. Priesthood is there, Royalty, the Prophetic Office, Sacrifice, Martyrdom—all alike are jewels which He confers on those who follow Him, each in His own degree. But, for the most part, we shall pass these by: we shall consider Him from that same standpoint as that from which we have considered Him throughout—as our own familiar Friend who trusted us, and who was rewarded by us with the Crown of Thorns; who yet is content to bear all this and a thousand Passions more, if at the end He can but persuade us that He loves us. He spoke Seven Words as He hung there on Calvary, and each tells us of His Friendship.

"*Father, forgive them, for they know not what they do.*"[91]

Our Friend has climbed the Hill; He has been stripped of His

---

[91] Luke xxiii: 34.

clothes and laid upon the Cross that He has carried from the steps of the Prætorium. The executioners prepare and choose the nails.... Those whose love He is seeking stand round looking down upon His upturned face. He, lying there, sees them, and sees behind them all those whom they represent—all those countless souls each one of whom He desires to win. And, as the hammer is lifted and falls, He utters His first Word. *"Father, forgive them, for they know not what they do."*

I. And is such a word as this possible? Is it possible even for Divine Charity to declare that "they know not what they do"? He had lived three years in public as their servant and friend; He had helped all who came to Him, fed the hungry, healed the sick, relieved the tormented. Not once was it known that any who came to Him was cast out. Even those whom the world regarded as worthless, the ruined wrecks of humanity, the publican and the harlot,—even those who had lost the world's undiscriminating friendship, found a friend in Him. All this was undeniable; it was even a matter of public notoriety. It was impossible to pretend that the world rejected Him because He rejected the world—impossible to urge that the world was in ignorance of His prodigal charity and large-heartedness. He has been a friend to all. One only excuse was urged—He was no friend at least to Caesar.

But what they did not know—and it was upon this that Divine Charity fastened as the one loophole through which they might escape—was that it was their God who had done all these things; that it was the Creator who had been so tender to the creature; that it was the Lord of Life even now whom they held beneath their hands. They thought that they were taking His Life from Him; they did not understand that He was laying it down of Himself. They thought that they were ending for ever a career of mercy which displeased them; they did not know that they were co-operating in a supreme climax of mercy. They knew not what they did.

They knew, then, that they were outraging a human friend, but not that they were slaying a Divine Friend. They knew that they were betraying a fellow-creature, that they were sinning against every code destinies of such a soul. We do not know the tense expectation with which Heaven waits upon our whims: we do not know how here, in these minute opportunities of every day, lie the germs of new worlds that may be born to God, or crushed in embryo by our carelessness. We finger the jewels He was given us, and forget that each is worth a King's ransom; we play, like children in the midst of a garden, trampling down the flowers which God can replace but can never restore....

For it is a Divine cause that we Catholics are crucifying every day; and a Divine Honour that we are insulting. If we could but see Him, here lies Jesus in our midst, with the marks of His agony upon Him, waiting for "one to comfort" Him, but He "found none."[92] He lies here, and we gossip and stare, and go our ways where the tragedy is done, when He hangs between heaven and earth, descended from the one and rejected by the other—our God whom we thought our slave, who desires to be our Friend.

Father, then, by this prayer of Thy crucified Son, forgive us also; for we know not what we do.

But, above all, is this ignorance of ours the more startling in that very aspect of the spiritual life with which we are concerned. We know how it is a constant experience of those who are Christians to meet with Jesus suddenly coming to them as a Friend. There is scarcely an instructed Christian, at least, anywhere, who, usually in his youth, though occasionally in more mature life, does not suddenly awaken to the fact that Christ desires more than mere obedience, mere faith, or mere adoration—that He desires such a Friendship with Himself that its inception is no less than a moral conversion. It is a wonderful and a beautiful sight to observe a soul in this manner becoming conscious—as a maiden becomes conscious that she is loved—of the heart-shaking fact that her God is her Lover. He comes, as to His own—and His own receives Him.

And yet, again and again, as in human love, so in Divine love, the romance wears off; and the soul which a few years ago centred all upon

---

[92] Ps. lxviii: 21.

Jesus Christ, a soul which reformed her life and arranged its details with the single object of growing more and more conformed to her Friend, which embraced devotion as her principal business, which concentrated her capacities and instincts for beauty, her interests, her emotions, her understanding, solely upon Him; which took a new start in life and a new centre from which to act; which sloughed off her sins almost without an effort in the sunlight of His Presence—such a soul as this, when a little while has passed, when the searching processes of the Purgative Way begin to sift her through, or when imagination becomes weary, or maturity dulls the keen emotions of adolescence, or when the dreary facts of the world begin to reiterate their claim to be the sole proper object of consideration—little by little such a soul as this, instead of tightening her hold upon her Friend, instead of clinging, even in a faith that amounts almost to a virtue of desperation, to that which has, as a matter of fact, been the most real and vital experience of her life, instead of seeking to transfer the image of Jesus from the romantic mood which has, it may be, passed, to the mature state which is now hers, instead of striving to cling to Him with her weakness, in place of the natural strength which has gone—instead, relinquishes the tremendous reality among the fairy-stories of her youth, and counts Him and His Friendship as among those illusions which, though natural to early years, must pass away as experience increases. She is still content, perhaps, to treat Him as her God, as the ideal of the human race, as the Saviour of men; but no longer as the Lover who desires her among ten thousand, as the Prince who has awakened her with a kiss, to whom, henceforward she must wholly belong. And yet so seldom it is that she knows what it is that she does! She regrets it, maybe, a little; she sees that it would have been more perfect to have persevered; she even envies, a little, those who have persevered. She knows that she has been wanting; but she knows not how much. She knows not that she has forfeited the possibility of sanctity, that she has missed for ever a thousand opportunities that can never come back: she knows not that, if it were not for God's mercy, she would have forfeited for a certainty even the probability of her salvation.

II

An hour perhaps has passed away.…The screams and the blasphemies of the two tortured thieves have died to moans, and the moans to the silence of exhaustion; and in the silence the Grace of God and the habits of the past have been at work together. The one on this side is still absorbed in his own pain, regarding it, contrasting it, turning it this way and that, seeking to adjust it: and the other is aware that there is something in the universe besides his own pain, that his pain is not the beginning and the end of all things. From time to time he has caught glimpses, as his head writhed this way or that, through blinding blood and tears, through the mist of dust trampled up by the surging crowds, of Another who hangs in the midst. His friend has seen Him too, but has seen His patience only as a reproach to His own torment.…"If thou be Christ, save Thyself, and us."[93] Yet this one sees more than a failure and a tragedy: he has heard, maybe, that first Word groaned out as the nails went through; and upon this detail and that and the other, his own darkened mind—the mind of a savage child—has been painfully at work.

And Grace has been at work too, in its mysterious operation, upon that defiled and undeveloped mind, like sunlight in a filthy slum.… We know almost nothing, after all our theology, of that Divine process; we know a little of its conditions, a fraction of its effects; we have labelled a few by-laws of its working; but no more. This, however, we know—that the man to whom it came was not wholly self-centred; that there was still in him enough receptivity for Grace to enter.

I. So, little by little, the truth—(we dare not say the whole explicit truth)—began to filter in. That darkened mind began to catch glimpses, that came and went and returned, of the supreme Fact which the cultivated Pharisees overlooked…that the Criminal was not wholly a Criminal, that the Thorns were not wholly a mockery, that the title above the Cross was something besides a sneer.…Pain is a strange

---

[93] Luke xxiii: 39.

magician when Grace stands behind, an initiator into secrets, a High Priest who handles and dispenses mysteries unknown to those who have not suffered....

At least we know that the thief spoke at last—a greater miracle than Balaam's ass!—that a murderer recognized the Lord of Life, that a liar spoke the truth, that an outlaw submitted to the King. "Lord, remember me when Thou shalt come into Thy kingdom."

He asks, therefore, for the least thing for which he could ask—that a King who will some day enter into a kingdom will not wholly forget that there is such a creature as Dismas, who once suffered by His side. He no longer submits a doubt—"*If* thou be the Christ"—but he calls Him "Lord" outright. He no longer asks for relief—"save Thyself and us"; but for some future remembrance. One day, whenever that may be, remember....

And, upon the word, the miracle happens which always happens when a soul begins with shame to take the lower place. As soon as we have learnt to be servants we receive the place and name of Friend. "Friend, go up higher."[94]... "I will not now call you servants...but I have called you friends."[95] For He is the One, *cui servire regnare est*; whose service is perfect freedom...."This day thou shalt be with Me in Paradise."[96]

II. Here, then, is one of the most profound laws of the spiritual life, and one of the most difficult to learn, because, like all the fundamental laws of grace, as well as of nature, it presents itself as a paradox."If you wish to be high, you must aim to be low."... "He that humbleth himself shall be exalted."[97]

(i) Now, as long as Self reigns within the soul, our whole instinct is, obviously, in some manner towards self-assertion, even though that object may be disguised in terms of the Love of God. Certainly a soul can win heaven by continuing to desire it effectively; but it is equally certain that a soul cannot reach the highest place in heaven, still

---

[94] Luke xiv: 10.
[95] John xv: 15.
[96] Luke xxiii: 43.

less the position of an intimate friend of Christ on earth, from such a motive as this. That is, so long as Self reigns, until Self has been denied and crucified, the soul cannot be, in the highest sense, Christ's disciple. We usually set out on our spiritual life, aiming to be proficient, to make progress, to accomplish something for God, to render ourselves, in a way, indispensable to the Divine Cause. We carry, that is to say, into spiritual things the same ambitions and emulations as serve to make a man eminent in worldly affairs. We attempt, in a sense, to force our friendship on Christ, and to insist on that relationship to Him on which we have set our heart. We seek to bend the Divine Will to ours, to accomplish our union with God by attempting to change Him rather than ourselves.

And we fail, of course, lamentably and ignominiously, every time. For in spiritual matters there must be a reversal of the usual methods, if there is to be success. Certainly "blessed are they that hunger"; blessed are they that are "ambitious"; but the ambition must be pursued not by self-assertion but by self-extinction; for "blessed are the meek"; "blessed are the poor in spirit"; "blessed are they that mourn."[98]

So, again and again, through a lack of the Christian spirit, even though we aim at the Christian life, we become disheartened and discouraged. We make no progress, and, even if we do not altogether give up the quest, we at least begin to falter in it.

(ii) But, on a sudden, the soul makes a blinding discovery; for the first time, perhaps, she sees Humility with her face unveiled, and in her eyes perceives the true image of herself. Then, in swift succession, follow discovery after discovery in addition. She understands, for example, that this self on which she has set her heart is simply not worth having; she perceives that there is not one of her good actions in the past that has been wholly good, for each that has not been done out of a merely natural generosity, has been done largely out of this very love of self; she learns that her "progress," for the most part, has been in the wrong direction altogether, that she has been accumulating merits

---

[97] Luke xiv: 11.
[98] Matt. v: 3 ff.

that have scarcely a touch of meritoriousness, that she has been serving self throughout in those very actions which she had told herself were pleasing to God; in short, that her development has lain only in an increase of self-centredness, and that the self-control that she has learned by her efforts has been a "vicious victory" (as St. Augustine calls it) after all; since she has been striving all along to conquer God, instead of yielding to Him.

Then, indeed, the cry breaks from her spontaneously, "Lord, remember me when Thou shalt come into Thy Kingdom.... Lord, remember me...forget not altogether that such as I exist, in that far-off day which I had thought in my pride was already past, that day when Thou shalt take Thy power and reign even in this heart that so long has been a rebel to Thee. Remember me, when the supreme achievement of love has been wrought, and Human Nature has been made conformable to the Divine.... Dear Jesus, in that day be to me not a Judge, but a Saviour!"

And then, by one more bewildering paradox, all is done; and the soul in that instant has what she desires. She has prayed that she may learn to serve, and with the very utterance of that prayer finds that she has been taught to reign. For she has learned the lesson of Him who was made in the form of a servant that He might rule kings—of Him who was meek and humble of heart—and she has found rest to her soul. For His arms are that instant about her, His kiss is on her lips, and His Words in her ear—"To-day thou shalt be with me in Paradise!" "O Soul that I have made and loved, who hast learnt at last to be my servant, come up higher, from my Feet to my Heart, O my friend! Now that thou hast at last put thyself at my mercy, behold! in that instant I put myself at thine. Take my hand and walk with me, now that thou art willing to follow me; for see—we walk together already in Paradise."...

Oh! this Friendship of Jesus for the Penitent! Just now there were three of Christ's intimates round His Cross—the immaculate Mary and the stainless disciple whom Jesus loved, upon the one side, with the purified weeping Magdalene upon the other. Now the quaternion of His lovers is complete, for the brokenhearted Thief has joined them—he who desired to serve, and therefore merited to reign.... And he, too, already hangs in Paradise.

III

Two of the personages standing beside the Cross are, for all Christians, for all time, the supreme types of Divine and human love. There is Mary, loved into immaculate being by the Eternal Father, the Mother Herself of Immaculate Love, and John the chosen disciple, allowed to rest his head, even before he had attained heaven, upon the breast of that same Immaculate Love. Surely these two, Mary and John, are already as wholly one as Love can make them. Those who love God so perfectly cannot love one another less perfectly.... Yet Jesus, in His seven words upon the Cross, devotes one to make them closer still.

I. Our Lord desires not merely to form Friendships between Himself and every human soul, but to unite friends in divine charity to one another. He makes in fact the bond of charity between men the final test of charity towards Himself. "He that loveth not his brother, whom he seeth, how can he love God, whom he seeth not?"[99] "As long as you did it not to one of these least, neither did you do it to me."[100] The second commandment is like "unto the first": "Thou shalt love thy neighbour as thyself."[101] If one half of the energies of His life on earth has been to draw men to Himself, the other half has been to draw men to one another. "By this shall all men know that you are my disciples, if you have love one for another."[102] He pronounces blessings, then, not merely on those who "hunger and thirst after Justice," after the Divine Fount of Justice, but upon the peacemakers and the meek; for those who forgive not one another their trespasses (those who do not make the Divine bond between them stronger than the human divisions that would separate them) cannot have their own trespasses forgiven—cannot, that is, rely upon a Divine bond which they them-

---

[99] I John iv: 20.
[100] Matt. xxv: 45.
[101] Mark xii: 31, Lev. xix: 18.

selves have repudiated.

II. Now the union of men with one another is, in one sense, the object of every human society. There has been verified gradually even in the most worldly spheres that fact which has always been preached by Christianity, that union is strength, that co-operation is better than competition, that to "lose self" in a Society of some kind is the only means of saving self; that individuality can be retained only by the sacrifice of individualism. But in practically all human societies that have ever existed, the bond of union is thought to be one of prosperity. "If we can rejoice together, win together, triumph together, we shall be able to love one another."

Now Jesus Christ does something that has never been done before. He uses suffering as the supreme bond of love. "Love one another," He cries from the Cross, "because you are strong enough to suffer together." "Mother," cries the dying Friend of us all, "behold thy son. Son, behold thy Mother!"

This word, then, is no less significant of an immense spiritual principle than are the rest. Mary and John have loved one another perfectly—as perfectly, that is to say, as a common joy has made possible. Together they have watched His triumph: Mary has seen Him, the Child of Joy, upon her breast: John upon His breast has seen Him rejoice in spirit. But, from to-day onwards, their common love rises to yet greater heights: they love one another now, not merely in the Sacred Heart, but *in the pierced and broken Sacred Heart*. Hitherto they have been perfect friends; henceforth they are Blood-relations—relations in a blood more intimate to them than their own—a Blood shed for the remission of sins. It is not, "Friend, behold thy friend"; but, "Mother, behold thy son. Son, behold thy Mother!"

III. (i) First, then, this is the bond which unites Mary to ourselves—not that she sang the *Magnificat*, but that the sword pierced her own heart also. Sorrow, wrongly received, is a mightier force than all ordinary human affections: sorrow, borne with resentment and bit-

---

[102] John xiii: 35.

terness, isolates the soul not only from God but from her own fellows. The wounded stag creeps away to die in loneliness. But, on the other hand, if sorrow is welcomed and taken in, if it is made, by the very effort which welcomes it, a bond of union with others that suffer, a link is forged which all the powers of hell cannot break. If Mary had been given us as our Mother in Bethlehem, if she had wrapped herself in her unique joy, if she had been to us but a figure of incarnate bliss; then when the horror of darkness fell upon us, we too should have crept away from even Her, to suffer in loneliness. A religion that presented to us Mary with her living child in her arms, and had no Mary with her dead Son across her knees, could not have been the religion to which we should turn in utter confidence when all else had failed. More—she could not have been our Mother in any but an adopted sense, if her bearing of us had been without pain. But, as it is, she who brought forth her unfallen First-born painlessly, brought forth the rest of her fallen Human Family in agony and darkness. Indeed she is the Mother of the redeemed, because she was the Mother of Redemption: she stood by the Cross of Jesus, as she had knelt by His cradle; and she is our Mother, then, by that very blood by which both she and we are alike redeemed. The "Mother of Sorrows" must always be nearer to the human race than even the "Cause of our Joy."

(ii) It is only too easy, so soon as we begin to make any progress in spiritual religion, to forget those simple elementary duties in which that religion began. Or, to put it another way, it is only too easy, when we have begun to experience an intimate and personal relationship with Jesus Christ, to forget, or at least to minimize, the relations that bind us to one another. Our Lord, therefore, in this Word directs our attention once more to the elementary fact that "he that loveth not his brother whom he seeth, cannot love God whom he seeth not," however fervid or ecstatic his emotions may seem. We have then, continually, to test the reality of our devotion to Him by our practical devotion to one another.

If ever, then, there is a time when it is proper for us to turn to one another, and to verify our charity, it is when we stand beneath the

Cross; since it is the supreme glory of the Cross that it claims to make suffering the deepest bond of human relations. Mahomet and Buddha lived to make men one: Buddha even, we are told, returned to earthly life to accomplish this. But it is Jesus Christ alone who died to unite them. Every earthly kingdom is troubled by sedition and faction so soon as it begins to totter: the Kingdom of God alone draws its bonds more closely as it approaches more nearly the extinction of Calvary.

This is the moment, then, when our souls are most exalted in watching our Saviour die, to turn from that sight to the most ordinary and simple relationships of everyday life, and to ask ourselves whether we have that final proof of our discipleship of Jesus—that we love one another. It is an appalling fact that again and again those who claim to be enjoying the most intimate friendship with God are distinguished by selfishness and a lack of charity towards their neighbours—that it is those, again and again, above all others who live what are called "misunderstood" lives, who actually advance their "Rule of Life" or the calls of their devotion as arguments against their having time or energy to be kind to their servants or acquaintances. "She is at her prayers, therefore she must not be disturbed. He is getting ready for the sacraments; therefore it is natural that he should be a little peevish and preoccupied."…

Go home, then, and make up that foolish quarrel once and for all: go home and apologize simply and sincerely for your share in that trouble in which perhaps the other was even more to blame than yourself. It is intolerable that the friends of the Crucified—that those even who aspire to be friends of the Crucified—should think it conceivable to be at peace with God, who are not at peace with wife or husband or parents.

"Behold your Mother…your son!" That soul with whom you are at variance has a bond with you far greater than that of a common creation. The fact that the Eternal Word died for you both upon the Cross is an infinitely stronger link of union than the fact that the Eternal Word willed you both into being. For while the Fall broke the harmony of creation, the Redemption restored it; and this restoration is a far greater marvel than even Creation itself.

No man can be a Friend of Jesus Christ who is not a friend to his neighbour.

IV

The darkness of Calvary, spiritual as well as physical, draws on to its deepest. Christ has prayed for those who have outraged and repudiated His Friendship: He who was always the Friend of Sinners has added one more to the company: He who was always the Friend of Saints has united two of them yet more closely than ever by the wedding of Pain. Now He draws inwards from the world for which He has done so much: He directs this consciousness into His own Sacred Humanity; and in a Word at which heaven and earth tremble together, reveals to us that that Sacred Humanity, as a part of that process by which He chose to "taste death for all"[103] and to learn "obedience by the things which He suffered,"[104] has to experience the sorrow of dereliction. He who came to offer that Sacred Humanity as the bond of Friendship between God and man, wills that His own Friendship with God should be obscured. He becomes indeed the Friend of fallen man, for He chooses to identify Himself with the horror of that Fall. The Beatific Vision which was lost to man through that fall, and which Jesus Christ can never lose, is now obscured to the eyes of Him who comes to restore it through Redemption.

I. Now, the true happiness of man consists in his gradual approach to the Beatific Vision. Christ offers us His Friendship on earth—that Friendship in which all human happiness consists—as a pledge and as a means of obtaining that final union with Him in heaven which we call by that name. Therefore the joy of Christ Himself on earth—that joy which again and again burst out into words during His earthly life, or into deeds of power and mercy, or into the silent radiance of the Transfiguration—that joy arose from the Beatific Vision on which He

---

[103] Heb. ii: 9.
[104] Heb. v: 8.

continually lived. He "endured as seeing Him that is invisible."[105]

It is now, on Calvary, that the supreme outrage takes place; that that which has been His support throughout His thirty years of life, the strength of that "meat" of which His disciples knew nothing,[106] has become, while not withdrawn, yet darkened to His eyes, together with every other consolation, human or Divine, that might, conceivably, have taken its place. The darkened sun above Him was a faint and shadowy type of His own darkened Soul. The sun is turned into blackness and the moon into blood and the stars fall from heaven, and the earth shakes, as, of His own free will and deliberate choice, He enters not merely into the shadow of death, but into the Death of deaths itself. It is this Death of which He "tasted.".... In this hour He puts from Him the one and only thing that makes life tolerable. His Body, torn and strained on the Cross, is but a very faint incarnation of the agony of His derelict Soul...."My God, my God! Why hast Thou forsaken me?"[107]

II. This Word is the one that, above all others, is most difficult of application to ourselves. For the state in which it was uttered is simply inconceivable to us who find our consolation in so much that is not God, and to whom sin means so little. If physical comforts are wanting to us, we find refuge in mental comfort; if mental comforts are wanting, we lean upon our friends. Or, more usually, when the higher pleasures are withdrawn, we find relief, with scarcely an effort, in lower. When religion fails us, we console ourselves with the arts; when love or ambition disappoint us, we plunge into physical pleasures; when the body refuses to respond, we take refuge in our indomitable pride; and when that in its turn crumbles to nothing, we look to suicide and hell as a more tolerable environment. There seems no depth to which we will not go, in our passionate determination to make ourselves tolera-

---

[105] Heb. xi: 27.
[106] John iv: 32.
[107] Matt. xxvii: 46.

ble to ourselves.

This Word, then, is meaningless to most of us; for to Jesus Christ, when the Beatific Vision was overlaid with sorrow, there was nothing in Heaven or upon earth.... "I looked for one that would grieve together with me, but there was none: for one that would comfort me, and I found none."[108]...The tragedy goes on, up there in the darkness: we hear the groan; we catch glimpses of the tortured, colourless Face behind which the Soul itself hangs crucified;...we grope, we conjecture, we attempt to form lower images of the august reality; but that is all.

Two great lessons, however, translated into terms that we can, perhaps, partly understand, come down to us:

(i) Occasionally even we ourselves rise to the point in the spiritual life where our Friendship with Christ is our chief joy, among all the other and lesser consolations that God gives. The fact that we know Him and can speak with Him is reckoned by us as sufficiently sweet as to make its apparent withdrawal the most acute of all our sorrows. (I need hardly say that this requires no particular proficiency in spiritual things. It is, in fact, impossible to be sincere and persevering in our religion, without sooner or later experiencing it.) Well, such a point is reached by us, let us say; and then, on a sudden, without our being conscious of anything more than our usual faithlessness and lethargy, this spiritual pleasure in religion is swiftly and completely withdrawn. And then what is our usual response?

As was remarked just now, a usual plan is instantly to find consolation elsewhere. We "distract" ourselves, as we say; we turn our attention to other things. But a yet commoner plan is to lose heart altogether, to give up the practices which cause us pain, and meanwhile to complain bitterly of the way in which our Friend is treating us. Certainly a cry of help is not only justifiable, but actually meritorious; for our Lord Himself so cried upon the Cross. The fault lies not in so crying, but in resenting while we cry. It seems to us, in our complacency, as if we

---

[108] Ps. lxviii: 21.

had deserved better of our Lord; as if there was a kind of right on our part to insist always upon the sense of our Friend's presence. Yet how, without such withdrawals, is progress possible? How is our hold upon our Friend to be tightened unless now and again it seems as if He were slipping from our grasp? How is real faith to throw out its roots and clench its fibres into the Rock, unless the desolating wind of trouble at times threatens to uproot us altogether? For the keener the tribulation and the more bitter the dregs, the more honourable is the draught. To hold our lips to that Cup which our Saviour drained, even though its bitterness is diluted by His mercy—the honour of this should surely be enough to make us hold our peace, for very shame.

(ii) A second lesson is, that the state in which God is the All of a soul, is a state to which we are bound at any rate to aspire. It is not enough that the Friendship of Christ should be merely the first of our various interests. Christ is not merely "the First"; He is Alpha and Omega, the beginning and the end. He is not the relatively most important; He is the Absolute and the All. Religion is not one of the departments which make up our life—(that is Religiosity)—but Religion is that which enters into every department, the fabric on which every device, whether of art or literature, or domestic interests, or recreation, or business, or human love, must be embroidered. Unless it is this, it is not Religion as it is intended to be.

To make it so, however, is the supreme difficulty of spiritual life—to make it, that is, not only an integral element in the whole of life, but the dominant element in every department—in such a sense that its claims are imperative always, everywhere; again, not in the sense that the soul is uninterested in everything except the actual forms of worship or theology or asceticism or morals—this again may be called religiosity, or at least a sort of professionalism—but in such a way that the Will or the Power or the Beauty of God is subconsciously perceived in everything, and that "nothing is secular, except sin."

Now this, let us remind ourselves, is actually intended to be the life of every human soul; and, in proportion as we approximate to it, we are more or less fulfilling our destiny. For it is only to a soul that has reached this state that God can be All. He becomes "All" because nothing is any longer alien to Him. "Whether you eat or drink or whatsoever else you do, do all to the glory of God."[109] The whole of life becomes illuminated with His Presence; everything is seen to subsist in Him: Nothing has any value except so far as it is in relations with Him....

This, then, is the state for which a Christian soul is bound to strive and aspire. This and this only is the entirety of the Friendship of Christ; to a soul in this condition, and to her alone, can Jesus truly be said to be All. And this, further, is the only state in which real "Dereliction" is possible. To lose Jesus if He occupies nine-tenths of our life surely brings extraordinary pain; but there yet will remain one-tenth in which the loss is not felt—one fractional interest to which the soul may turn for consolation. But when He occupies the whole of life, when there is not one moment of the day, one movement of the senses, one perception or act of the mind in which He is not the background—subconsciously perceived and apprehended at the least—then, indeed, when He withdraws Himself, the sun is darkened and the moon cannot give her light; then indeed the savour goes out of life, and the colour fades from the sky, and form vanishes from beauty, and harmony from sound. It is such a soul as this, and this only, who can dare without presumption to take on her lips the words of Christ Himself, and to cry, "My God, my God, why hast Thou forsaken me? For in losing Thee, I lose all."

V

The agony of Christ's Soul is passing, and the agony of the Body reasserts itself. He has hung since morning in the blaze of sunlight, sheltered only for a while by the darkness which hid the torment of His Soul; and as the minutes have gone by, little by little, like a tide of fire, has risen that thirst of Crucifixion which, some tell us, is the extremest pain of the sharpest form of death.

---

[109] I Cor. x: 31.

I. (i) Up to the present the deepest point of Christ's Humiliation has been His cry to His Father—that call for help by the Sacred Humanity which by His own Will was left derelict—His confession to the world that His Soul was in darkness. Now, however, He descends a still deeper step of humiliation, and calls for help, to man.

Christ asks man to help Him!

All through His life He had offered help: He had fed hungry souls and hungry bodies. He had opened blind eyes and deaf ears; and lifted up the hands that hung down, and strengthened the feeble knees. He had stood in the Temple and called to all that thirsted to come and drink. Now, in return, He asks for drink, and accepts it. So David, too, in the stress of battle had cried, "Oh that some man would give me a drink of the water out of the cistern that is in Bethlehem!"[110] For both David and David's Son were strong enough to condescend to weakness.

(ii) In the age-long Calvary of the world's history, Jesus cries on man to help Him; and the Giver of all humiliates Himself to ask.

Truly He makes every other appeal first. To the selfish undeveloped soul He speaks in the Voice of Sinai—"Thou shalt not." To a soul that has made a little progress He offers encouragement and promises. "Blessed is such and such a man, for he shall receive a reward." But here and there are souls that are deaf to Hell and Heaven alike, to whom the future means little or nothing—souls that are too reckless to fear Hell, too loveless to desire Heaven. And to those He utters His final heart-piercing appeal. "If you will not accept help from me, give at least help to me. If you will not drink from my hands, give me at least drink from yours. *I thirst.*"

It is an amazing thought that men should have reduced Him to this; and it is a suggestive thought that men who will not respond for their own sakes, will, sometimes, respond for His.

"See," cries Jesus Christ, "you have given up the search; you have turned away from the door and will not knock. You will not take the

---

[110] II Kings xxiii: 15.

trouble to ask. So it is I who have to do these things. Behold, it is I who go seeking the lost; it is I who stand at the door and knock. It is I who ask—who am become a beggar.... Have mercy upon me, O my friends, for the Lord hath afflicted me! I no longer offer water; but I ask it; for without it I die."

II. It is good for us then, sometimes, to look at the spiritual life from another standpoint altogether. There come moments and even periods in our lives when religion becomes an intolerable burden; when the search is so long and fruitless that we sicken of it; when no door opens, however vehemently we knock; when we ask, and there is no Voice that answers. At times like this we lose heart altogether. It seems to us even that our own desires are not worth satisfying; that religion, like every instinct of our nature, reaches an end beyond which there is no going; that desire has, in fact, failed, and that we are not even ambitious of attaining heaven. The truth is that we are limited beings; and that the "divine discontent," the desire for the infinite, the endless passion for God, is as much a grace from God as the power to reach to Him and win Him. It is not only that God is our reward, and our Lord; but He must actually be our Way by which we come to Him: we cannot even long for Him without His help.

It is when we are wearied out then by desiring, when desire itself has failed, that Jesus speaks to us in this Fifth Word from the Cross.

We have spoken of the Divine Friendship throughout as if it were a mutual relationship, as if we on one side, and Christ on the other, were united in a common bond. But, as a matter of fact, it is all on one side. We cannot even desire Christ without, except by the help of Christ within. The Christ within must cry "I thirst,"[111] before the Christ without can give us the Living Water.

This appeal, then, of Jesus must be our last and final motive, when all other impulses have failed. He is so beaten and rejected that He is come even to this. He must ask for mercy upon Himself, before He can have mercy on us. If we do not find our Heaven in Him, at least let Him find His Heaven in us. If we can no longer say, "My soul is athirst for the Living God," at least let us listen when the Living God cries,

"My Soul is athirst for you." If we will not let Him minister to us, for very shame let us be content to minister to Him.

III. This then is, again, the cry that goes up ceaselessly from Christ in His Church. We live in days that are full of terror and menace. Once the Church ruled in Europe; she was acclaimed as "coming in the Name of the Lord." She went about doing good, offering the Water of Life, and giving it—the Bread of Life, and distributing it. Now before our eyes she is going on her Way of Sorrows; she is climbing the Hill; she is hanging on the Cross.... The world has won, once more;—has won exactly so far as it won on Calvary. Men no longer allow her to minister to them; more, they will not even allow her to minister to herself. They have nailed her to emblems of secular government; taken away her glory; and taunted her, that she cannot be the Saviour of others, since she cannot even save herself.

What hope then is left? How can hands bless that are nailed fast? How can fettered feet go to seek those that are lost? How can lips, bruised and parched with desolation, preach the tidings of divine liberty?

Yet she can still cry out in pain *for her own sake*. She can go on uttering cry after cry —in France, for the right to quench the thirst that will be her death if it is not satisfied; in Italy and Portugal, for the bare right to exist in the midst of a society which she brought forth and nursed to maturity....

And, for our own comfort, let us remember that it is Jesus Himself who so cries; and that when, once for all, He first uttered His petition, by the side of Jacob's well, and on the Cross of Calvary—even the Samaritan woman, the alien from God's commonwealth, even the soldiers of an Empire that was at war with God's kingdom, had mercy upon Him, and gave Him to drink.

---

[111] John xix: 28.

VI

The evening light begins to glimmer again upon Calvary, the three crosses, and the little group that waits for the end; and as it falls upon the Face of Christ, the look of agony is gone. He has cried alike to God and man to have pity, upon tortured Soul and parched Body, and each has answered. Now in that Face, bleached by the darkness of the soul, and the Eyes, sunken with sorrow, a new look begins, that rises, as those who stand by watch Him, until the whole Face is radiant once again. The breaths come fuller and fuller, the Body nailed by its extremities begins to lift itself higher and higher till strength is regained sufficient for Him not to speak only, but to utter a cry so loud and triumphant as to startle and amaze the officer who has watched many men die, but never as This Man dies. The cry peals out, like the shout of a king in the moment of victory; and, in an instant, failure and labour and bitterness are behind Him for ever. *Consummatum est....* "It is finished!"[112]

I. Christ came into the world to accomplish the greatest work of all—greater than that sheer act of the Divine Will by which all things came into being out of nothing, greater than that steady output of Divine Energy by which all things are held in being, the stars in their courses, atoms in cohesion, and the worlds of flesh and spirit in their mutual relations. For it is a greater act to restore than to create, to bring the disobedient will back to obedience than to will it into existence, to reconcile enemies than to create worshippers, to redeem than to make. That God should make man is an act of power; but to redeem him is an act of Love....

The whole of history up to Calvary is, looked at from one side, one ceaseless effort of preparation for Redemption. Not one lamb has shed his blood in vain, not one prophet has spoken, not one king has reigned, except as a link in that chain of which the Lamb of God, the Servant of the Lord, and the King of Kings, is the end and the climax

---

[112] John xix: 30.

that justifies the whole. Abraham saw His day, and was glad; David sang of the day of His birth and of His wounded hands and feet: Isaias spoke of His grave with the wicked and his resting-place in the rich man's garden. God has brought all up to this point that crowns and fulfils them all. And now, *Consummatum est.*

Again, as we look back to Calvary through two thousand years, we see that all that God has done since, takes its rise from there; that every impulse of grace, every sacrifice and prayer offered, every movement of the Spirit of God, every response from the spirits of men, every sin forgiven, every new life begun, every death of a righteous man, every birth of a new soul into innocence—all these gain their full strength and indeed their very existence from the torrent of love that burst up into being at the foot of Christ's Cross.

Therefore at this moment, as the last drop of the Precious Blood is passing from His broken Heart, with a power beyond that of a dying man, Jesus cries in triumph, "It is finished."

Friendship between God and man is now made possible again, in the Body of Christ. That old irreconcilable enmity between the sin of the creature and the Justice of the Creator, between the defilement of the spirit and the Holiness of the Father of Spirits, is done away. We can be "accepted in the Beloved."

First, then: salvation is open to the sinner. No sin henceforth is unforgivable. Charity, it has been said, is the pardoning of the unpardonable and the loving of the unlovable: and in this Precious Blood, as the prophet sang, "there shall be a fountain open for the washing of the sinner and of the unclean";[113] and as the apostle wrote, it is this Blood which "cleanseth us from all sin."[114] The Friendship of God, therefore, is flung wide open to every soul that desires it.

But, more than this. Not only is mere friendship made possible by the death of Christ, but degrees of friendship to which even the angels cannot aspire. It is not only that a soul, through the Precious Blood, can pass from death to life, but that she can pass up through stages and heights and strata of that life, up to the perfection of sanctity itself. David could thirst for God; David could look on and up to that "awakening in the likeness of God" which is the soul's supreme satisfaction; but not until Christ had died could a soul reach that final object of the Divine desire and of her own which now lies open to every soul that is content to make the sacrifices necessary to gaining it. Not only, in the power of the Precious Blood, and the grace of the sacraments liberated by Its shedding, can every action, word and thought be brought into obedience to Christ, but the soul can, by that same grace, reach a point of union with Him so vital and so complete that she can truly cry "with Christ I am nailed to the Cross. And I live, now not I; but Christ liveth in me."[115]

II. Christ's work, then, is "finished" on the Cross—finished, that is, not as closed and concluded, but, as it were, liberated from the agonizing process which has brought it into being—finished, as bread is finished from the mills and the fire, that it may be eaten; as wine is finished after the stress and trampling of the winepress—finished, as a man's body is finished in the womb of his mother and brought forth with travail.

It is finished, that is, for a new and glorious Beginning, that the stream which has flowed from His Wounds may begin to flood the souls of men, and the Flesh that has been broken, feed them indeed. For now the Passion of Christ begins to be wrought out in His Mystical Body, and she to "fill up those things that are wanting of the Sufferings of Christ."[116] Now the enormous Process that has crushed and mangled Him in His assumed Nature begins effectively to carry on that same work of Redemption in the Human Nature of His Church, which, mystically, is the Body in which He dwells always—One Sun sets in order that another sun, which is yet the same, may begin to run his course. "The evening and the morning are one day."

And yet, we His friends—we, who in virtue of His Friendship are enabled to live, to die and to rise in union with Him—live for the most part as if He had never died. Compare the life of a cultivated fas-

---

[113] Zach. xiii:1.
[114] I John i: 7.
[115] Gal. ii: 20.

tidious pagan with the life of a cultivated fastidious Christian. Draw the two from corresponding classes and set them side by side. Is there so enormous a difference? There are a few differences in the religious emblems of the two. The one has an Apollo; the other a Crucifix. The one has the Egyptian goddess with her son in her arms; the other has the Immaculate Mother of Jesus with her Holy Child. Their talk is different, their dresses, their houses—all those external matters that are wholly indifferent to the soul's life. But are their virtues so different, their outlook on eternity, their sorrow beside open graves, their hopes beside new cradles?...Even before Christ died, children loved their parents and parents their children. Do Christians rise so much higher now—nearer to that yet more amazing degree of love by which a man "hates his father and mother" in order to be the disciple of His Lord? Even before Christ died, chastity was a virtue. Are we so far advanced now in that purity of heart without which no man can see God? Even a Roman Emperor once preached self-control, and practised it. Are our own houses any better models of the peace of brethren who dwell together in unity?

Did Christ finish His work, merely in order that society might decay no further?...God help us! As we look at what is called Christian Society to-day, it seems as if Christ had not even yet begun.

Yet here is this vast river of grace pouring from Calvary, the river that ought to be making glad the City of God. Here is this enormous reservoir of grace, bubbling up in every sacrament, soaking the ground beneath our feet, freshening the air we breathe. And we still in our hateful false humility talk as if Perfection were a dream, and Sanctity the privilege of those who see God in glory.

In Christ's Name, let us *begin*. For Christ has *finished*.

VII

Our Lord has just cried aloud that Sixth Word in which He proclaimed that there was finished at last that "Father's business" of which

---

[116] Col. i: 24.

He had first spoken in the Temple. Now He droops His Head again little by little upon His Breast, and in the words that he had learned at Mary's knee—words in which every Jewish child committed the care of his soul into God's care through the coming night—He commits His spirit into His Father's hands. For the evening is drawing on and the Sabbath is near in which once more, God, having seen all that He has done, pronounces it "Very good" and rests from His labours.

I. The thought of this Peace of Death into which our Divine Friend is passing is one of the most moving considerations of the Passion. He has been about His work for thirty-three years; and not for one instant, since He first drew mortal breath in the frosty stable of Bethlehem, has He ever yet truly rested. Even while He slept His Heart waked.

For that labour of His has included among other things the laying of foundations for the reform of the whole world. The whole of civilization, if it is to survive, the iron progress of the Roman Empire, the developing instincts of barbarian nations—all must remodel itself on the basis that He has laid down, or cease to exist. More than this: He has been laying down the constitution of a greater Kingdom than ever the world has seen—that Supreme supranational Society from which Kings must draw their sanctions and republics their right to command; for the successor of His Vicar is to be "Father of Princes and Kings and Lord of the World." And meanwhile His countless acts of mercy must be done; not one yearning soul must be sent empty away; not one sick body left uneased; not one transitory need, unsatisfied. And *He is Man* who has done all this. True, it is God alone who could have done it. No reformer, no philosopher, no monarch has ever even dreamed of founding such a Kingdom as this. But it has been accomplished through Human Nature; it has been the lips of a mortal Man who has said all these things; mortal hands that have laid those foundations; a mortal brain that has had to deal with and translate into human language and act the dreams of a God that must come true. Truly God cannot become weary; but God made man can become weary a thousand times over.

How utterly then has He earned His Rest! And at last He is to find it. The Soul through which such strong agonies have passed, is to sink into that peaceful place of refreshment and light where the souls that have served God according to their graces are awaiting that First Advent of their Redeemer. The Body that has borne so great a burden and heat of the day, that has been wearied with labours, and bowed down by sorrows—and, at last, has been beaten, pierced and broken by the hands of those for whom such labours were borne—this Body of His is to be laid in the cool rock-tomb, with wrappings of soft linen, soaked in spices and myrrh, to await once more the inbreathing of the Divine Energy which again shall pass through every vein, sinew and muscle, transforming each utterly back again to the unmarred Divine Image, in which, once again, now no longer subject to any law of limitation or weariness and waste, the Soul that can never sorrow again, shall eternally rejoice.

Our Friend sleeps at last.

II. The Peace of God that passes all understanding is by far His greatest gift, beyond health or wealth,—beyond, in a sense, all virtues themselves, since it is their crown and their final reward. It is this Peace in Christ that is the one thing needful, as He Himself tells us: it is that "good part," better than all activities and energies which "shall not be taken away."

It is this for which we look at death—the one hope that reassures and reconciles us to that violent cessation of activities which is to an energetic and vital soul the chief imaginative horror of death. It is even sometimes (so great is its attraction)—we might almost say that it must be—for every soul that is really taking part in the conflict of life, the chief attraction of death. For life must become from time to time an all but intolerable strain—not only is there that weariness of body which arises from its incapacity to rise always to the demands of the soul; but there is that further weariness of soul arising from its effort to respond always as it ought, to the excitations and demands of grace. If it only were possible, we cry, to cease from striving, to rest wholly on God without even an effort of the will, to relax and to sink into Him who alone is our Rest. And yet we must not; for this is *Quietism*—that strangely seductive system which means relaxation and lethargy—that drowsy sleep of a soul that is created that it may act, of a will that must actively adhere, so long as it can merit or demerit at all. It is only in the "divine necessity" of Purgatory that such a state is possible; and then, only, because it is necessary.

Yet there is a Peace of God even while we live; and it is for lack of this Peace that so many souls fret and beat themselves to Death against the encaging bars of their own limitations.... And it must come from one thing and one thing only, namely, a perfect balance in the environment for which our souls were made—not as of a bird sleeping on the water, but of a bird poised in the air—a perfect response, that is to say, on the part of our loving and lovable nature to the one adorable Nature which alone can support and can understand us—in a word, that Peace can alone be found in that of which we have been treating throughout, in an intimate, intelligent, affectionate and voluntary Friendship with Christ, who made us for Himself, and designed His own Incarnation that the union might be complete.

Activities, then, are good and necessary in their proper place. God's work cannot be done without them. But it is absolutely vital that, if these activities are to accomplish their objects, the soul engaged in them must possess Interior Peace. We go to and fro; we succeed or we fail; and it does not greatly matter which, since we have no final standard in this world by which we may estimate the one or the other. But Interior Peace is necessary; since our true "life is hid with Christ in God"[117]—that Peace which, He Himself tells us, the world can neither give nor take away—a Peace, that is, which, unlike other satisfying emotions, is wholly independent of external things. It is this Peace into which Christ Himself entered, body and soul, when He committed His Spirit into His Father's hands—that Sabbath Peace which He first inaugurated, and which "remaineth...for the people of God."[118]

Death is no longer frightful; and Life is no longer burdensome. For beneath the chilling stillness of death and the maddening rush of life, Christ and the soul dwell together in that tiny chamber of the heart, hewed out in that which is harder than any rock. It is not this rock that is rent when the graves are opened, and terrors stalk to and fro, and all Jerusalem is in panic; but here at last, when we have learned to die to all save Christ, when He is our All, He also is our Peace.

Let us look up for the last time at that Sacred Body hanging on the Cross. The Blood is all run out, the Soul is departed, and our Friend is at rest. Then let us go, that we may be buried with Him. And may our own souls, and the souls of all the faithful, both living and departed, rest in Him!

---

[117] Col. iii: 3.
[118] Heb. iv: 9.

13

EASTER DAY

Christ Our Friend Vindicated

Do not touch me, for I am not yet ascended to my Father. —JOHN xx: 17.

WE HAVE WATCHED DURING THIS PAST week the supreme tragedy of the world's history, presented with all possible splendour of liturgical and symbolical art. As the days have gone by we have seen our Friend as the central figure of a central drama, surrounded by a chorus of prophets, soldiers, priests, women, children—enemies and friends—in fact, by representatives of the whole human family of which He made Himself a member, each playing his appropriate part, each leading up along his own line, first to the dark and clear-cut grouping round the Cross and then to those flitting shadowed scenes, alight with mystical glory, by which the Catholic Church presents to us the eternal spiritual effects of Christ's Passion and Death. From the Divine side the story is one of triumph; from the human side one of failure—as, indeed, is the whole world's history throughout its entire course.

One by one the Secular Powers have gathered against Him, and one by one they have united together—interests at first antagonistic, and finally made friends together. Nationalism, denying the unity of the Human Family; Imperialism, denying the unity of the Divine Family; and, last, Worldly Religion that denies the appeal to the supernatural and the Transcendence of God. Herod, Pilate and Caiphas stand together at last, and Jesus is their enemy. This is the world's tragedy, therefore: "He came unto His own, and His own received Him not."[119] All this we have watched, up to the last final insult of sealing

---

[119] John i: 11.

the stone and setting the watch, not lest Christ should rise again (for "miracles do not happen!"), but for fear that His discredited followers should feign that it was so,—lest they should trouble the world's peace by one more religious fraud. Well! Let them alone! Our business is not with them to-day. They can work out their own theories in peace. Our affair to-day is not with the putting of Christ's enemies under His feet, but with the restoring of Christ to His friends' arms; with the vindication of Christ as our Divine Friend in whom we trusted and have not been disappointed; not with His final forcible manifestation to the world....

Let us watch that process, then, through the eyes of the humblest of His friends—one who was far from possessing the serene clear-sightedness of Mary His mother, or the desperately quiet confidence of the disciple whom He loved—but one who at least had to her credit, in spite of her sins against the Interior Voice and even against the decency of the world, that she "loved much," and "did what she could"—two simple virtues to which even the lowest of His lovers can aspire.

I. There were three great moments in the life of Mary Magdalene, after she had been brought into contact with Jesus Christ—moments that for sheer heart-shaking emotion can never be surpassed—three relationships with our Lord in which her hope was first raised to heaven, and then dashed down to the very edge of hell.

(i) First, Christ was her Absolver. The scene has been reproduced again and again in art and literature. The long tables are set out on the platform raised above the street, and the guests are seated. Down there in the lowest place, His feet still dusty from the roads, His hair dry and tangled with the wind, lies the Friend of all the world upon His couch, the young Carpenter from the north, invited here not so much to be honoured as to be examined and looked at, since He has succeeded in getting a certain notoriety among certain kinds of people.... And the great doctors of the Law are here, prudent, venerable-looking men, grave and dignified, talking quietly and earnestly, now to their host, now to one another. The servants go to and fro, in and out of the doorways behind, bringing in the courses and pouring wine. There, up from the street, comes the outcast, penitent indeed, but unforgiven—her long hair dishevelled on her shoulders, her saffron dress disordered, her pot of perfume in her hands. She has come, thinking perhaps it is her last chance—just to see Jesus, if no more, to look on Him who has looked kindly on her in the past, to see perhaps one glance of sorrow from those piercing eyes. The rest follows quickly. Almost before the servants have seen her, she is down there on the floor behind His couch, moaning gently in her misery, pierced through and through once more by the glance of the Divine Eyes. A silence falls as, unconscious of all except herself and Him, she droops her head so low that the tears drip on to His feet; and as, shocked at her own defilement of those sacred feet, she first wipes them frantically with her long hair, and then, as if to compensate for the touch of her tears, wrenches open the pot of perfume and dashes out the nard—the world's whispering begins, up there in the places of honour.

Jesus lifts His Head; and then, in a sentence or two, all is done.

"Thou seest this woman... She at least has done what thou, my host, didst leave undone... She loved much. She loved much... And therefore her sins are forgiven. Go, my daughter, and my friend. Sin no more."

(ii) With the memory of all this in her mind, as she looks back a few months later—months of a changed life, clean and sweet at last—conceive those raging tumultuous thoughts, agonies and hopes, as she follows step by step the torments and disgrace of Him who had absolved her and given her hope. She has followed since dawn every detail of His suffering. She has hung in the outskirts of the roaring crowd; has listened to the talking of those near her; she has heard the roar of laughter as He, her Friend, came out on to the steps, in the torn soldier's cloak, with the reed in His bound Hands and the mockery of the thorns on His Head. She has listened in the silence to the cutting slap of the scourge....Then she has followed Him again, through the streets, out through the gate, and up the little steep ascent. And, at last, when all is done, and He hangs there, stripped and shamed and tormented, and the soldiers have broken the line and fallen out into the crowd, she has pushed her way through, fought even to the foot of the quivering tree, and once more has "done what she could"...Once more she has washed those feet with her tears; and there, running down together on to the ground, there has flowed a sweeter stream than any that waters Paradise—the tears of the pardoned sinner and the Blood of the Saviour.

Yet how she must have hoped against hope, throughout, that the tragedy would not end tragically! She had seen Him before in the hands of His enemies and yet He had escaped. Even now as she crouched by the Cross, it was not altogether too late. He was not yet dead!... Where were those legions of angels of which He had spoken? Where, above all else, was that Divine Power that had comforted her, a power so evidently superhuman that there could be no limits to its achievements? As the roar swelled up from the crowd, "If Thou be the Son of God, come down from the Cross and we will believe," how she must have stared up into the quiet tormented Face with closed eyes that hung against the sky. And above all, when the roar had died away and from the two crosses on either side, from men, who because of their misery had a supreme claim on the Friend of Sinners, came the same screaming appeal, with its terrible addition, "If Thou be Christ, save Thyself—*and us*"—surely we may see her too spring to her feet, her hope once more strong within her that now at least He must answer. Surely at last that Power will vindicate itself, even at the eleventh hour; and the nails will burst into gems and the cross into flower, and He, her Friend, radiant again, will come down from His throne to receive a world's adoration! Is it possible that she herself, standing there, looking to Mary and John for encouragement, and then back again at Himself, whispered in her agony, "*Since* Thou art the Christ, save Thyself—*and me?*"

..."And Jesus cried with a loud voice and gave up the ghost...."

(iii) There is one thing left to her. Her Absolver is gone, her King is dead; but enough of her Friend is left to her for her still to be able to weep; for no soul can weep that has not still some capacity for joy.

Once more she who "loved much," "does what she can." She follows, step by step, to the quiet garden, after that for the last time she has washed Him with her tears and seen the ointments poured out; and she sees the stone rolled over the darkness within—a darkness which holds now that which for ever will make to her this garden a sanctuary of friendship....Then after a night and a day and a night she comes again in the dawn to visit her shrine.

The world has taken from her everything that can give her happiness. Not only are the joys of the world once for all impossible for her now, but even her new-found faith and hope and love are darkened: since He who had awakened them proved unable to save even Himself. Yet there is one thing which the world can never take—the memory of a Friendship so keen as to be a torment—Friendship itself even in the present. So long as she has the garden where His Body lies, she is content to live. Here she can come week by week as to the shrine of a God; she can watch the seasons come and go, and the grasses creep about the tomb; she still possesses something more dear to her than all the world has ever been.

This morning she will see Him, for the last time; and she walks quickly and silently, bearing in her hands once more the perfumes to anoint Him with....And then the last and most bitter blow of all strikes down—for the stone is gone, and in a pale light she sees within that the slab of stone is empty.... What then are these angels to her, whom she sees presently through her blinding desperate tears? It is not angels who can comfort her for the loss of the body of a human Friend.

"They have taken away my Lord," she sobs, "and I know not where they have laid Him." There is a step behind her; and she, "supposing him to be the gardener," pours out that same heart-broken lamentation to the man whom she cannot see.

"Sir, if thou hast taken Him hence, tell me where thou hast laid Him; and I will take Him away."

"Mary!"

"Rabboni!"

But there is still one more lesson for her to learn.

As she throws herself forward, speechless with love and desire, to grasp His Feet—to assure herself even by touch that it is these same feet indeed which she kissed in the Pharisee's house, and on the Cross of Calvary—that it is Himself, and no phantom—He moves back from her.

"Do not touch me, for I am not yet ascended to my Father."

"Do not touch me."…That Friendship is not what it used to be: it is infinitely higher. It is not what it used to be, since the limitations of that Sacred Humanity are gone—those limitations by which It was here and not there; by which It could suffer and grow weary and hunger and weep—limitations that endeared It to Its lovers, since they could indeed minister to It, comfort It, and hold It up. And Its expansion in Glory is not yet consummated—"I am not yet ascended to my Father"—that expansion of the Ascension and the Nine Days' Journey through the Heavenly Hierarchy, from the position "a little lower than the angels" to the Session and Coronation at the right Hand of the Majesty on high—that expansion of which the Descent of the Holy Ghost is the expression, and the Sacramental Presence of that same Humanity on a hundred altars the result.

And then, Mary, the Friendship shall be given back in "good measure and pressed down and shaken together and running over."[120] Then that which thou hast known on earth confined by time and space shall be given back to touch and handling once more. Again thy Friend shall be thine own. The Creator of Nature shall be present in that Nature, unlimited by its limitations. He who took Humanity shall be present in Humanity. He who spoke on earth "as one having authority" shall speak again in the same accent. He who healed the sick shall heal them in the Gate called Beautiful; He who raised the dead shall raise Dorcas in Joppa; He who called Peter in Galilee, shall call Paul in Damascus. A Friend again He shall be, as never before: a Creature exercising the power of the Creator: a Creator clothed with the sympathy of the

---

[120] Luke vi: 38.

Creature; God suffering on earth, and Man reigning in Heaven. But a Friend, first and last, in Alpha and Omega; a Friend who has died in the humiliation of Friendship; who has risen and reigns in its Eternal Power.

We have considered throughout Jesus Christ as our Friend. Let us on this day of His Vindication once more remind ourselves of a little of what this means.

He is first the Friend in the interior soul—that light that first blinds and then illuminates the eyes that look on Him, that they too may shine as the Light of the World.

But that interior friendship is but a part of what He offers; for, as once, two thousand years ago, He came out upon the stage of history, so He lives also to-day upon that same stage. The Christ who is within cries to the Christ without, that Christ may be all in all.

First, then, He lives in the Sacrament of His Love—as our Friend, our Sacrifice and our Food —and all three for friendship's sake.

Then, in another mode He lives in His Church on earth; in such a sense that the soul that hears Her hears Him, and the soul that despises Her despises Him; since she is His Body of which He is the Soul; since she has "the Mind of Christ," speaks (as He did) as "one having authority," and does "greater works" than did He "because He is gone to His Father" and therefore can live in her. It is to the lips of her Head, then, that His Friends listen, for this human Head is He to whom the Good Shepherd committed the pastorate of His Flock, to whom the "Door" entrusted "the keys"; whom the "One Foundation" named "the Rock."

Then, in yet another mode He lives in His Saints and supremely in His Blessed Mother. It is to these chosen Friends of God that we go to learn what is Friendship; to His Mother that we go to learn about her Son; to the Queen of Heaven, to learn the dispositions of the King.

And he lives, too, in His own dear sinners; in those who from their darkness teach us what light must be; in those who, crying in the wilderness in sin, make us keen-sighted in our despair on their behalf to seek the Shepherd who comes to seek them.

And He lives, too, by representation, in "the least of these His brethren" whom He commissions to beg and to hunger in His Name—in ordinary men who know but that they are ordinary, but who yet are made in His image, and, from their very fidelity to type, are true representatives of Him who claimed to be "Son of Man." And He lives in the sufferer, and the child; in the common task and the daily round; and He lives in the sunlight and the breeze, in the storm and the calm, in the tiny confines of earth, and the illimitable splendours of space; in the grain of sand as in the Sun; in the dew of the morning and the hugeness of the sea.

There is not one avenue of sense or thought, but the Figure of Christ stands in it; not one activity open to man, but the "Carpenter's Son" is there; beneath the stone, and in the heart of the wood.

The more minute our search, the more delicate is His Presence. The more wide our vision, the more illimitable is His Power.

So, little by little as we go through life, following with a hundred infidelities and a thousand blunders, with open defiances and secret sins, yet following, as Peter followed through the glare of the High Priest's fire to the gloom of penitence where Christ's Eyes could shine—as we go, blinded by our own sorrow, to the ecstasy of His Joy, thinking to find Him dead, hoping to live on a memory, instead of confident that He is living and looking to the "to-day" in which He is even more than yesterday—little by little we find that there is no garden where He does not walk, no doors that can shut Him out, no country road where our hearts cannot burn in His company.

And, as we find Him ever more and more without us, in the eyes of those we love, in the Voice that rebukes us, the spear that pierces us, the friends that betray us, and the grave that waits for us: as we find Him in His Sacraments, in His Saints—in all those august things which He Himself designed as trysting-places with Himself; at once we find Him more and more within us, enwound in every fibre of our lives, fragrant in every dear association and memory, deep buried in the depths of that heart of ours that seems most wholly neglectful of Him.

So, then, He asserts His dominion from strength to strength; claiming one by one those powers that we had thought to be most our own. To our knowledge He is the Most Perfect; to our imagination He is our dream; to our hopes their Reward.

Until at last, following His grace towards glory, we pass to be utterly His. No thought is ours unsanctioned by the Divine Wisdom; no love is ours save that of the Sacred Heart; no will save His.

"To me," then, "to live is Christ; and to die is gain."[121]... For "I live, now not I; but Christ liveth in me."[122]

My Friend is mine at last. And I am His....

---

[121] Phil. i: 21.
[122] Gal. ii: 20.

ABOUT THE CENACLE PRESS
AT SILVERSTREAM PRIORY

An apostolate of the Benedictine monastery of Silverstream Priory in Ireland, the mission of The Cenacle Press can be summed up in four words: *Quis ostendit nobis bona*—who will show us good things (Psalm 4:6)? In an age of confusion, ugliness, and sin, our aim is to show something of the Highest Good to every reader who picks up our books. More specifically, we believe that the treasury of the centuries-old Benedictine tradition and the beauty of holiness which has characterized so many of its followers through the ages has something beneficial, worthwhile, and encouraging in it for every believer.

cenaclepress.com

Also available:

Robert Hugh Benson
Confessions of A Convert

Robert Hugh Benson
The King's Achievement

Robert Hugh Benson
By What Authority

Blessed Columba Marmion OSB
Christ the Ideal of the Monk

Blessed Columba Marmion OSB
Christ in His Mysteries

Blessed Columba Marmion OSB
Words of Life On the Margin of the Missal

Dom Hubert Van Zeller OSB
Letters to A Soul

Dom Hubert Van Zeller OSB
We Work While the Light Lasts

Visit cenaclepress.com for our full catalog.